The Oxford English Programme 1

John Seely
Frank Green
David Kitchen

Steve Barlow
Richard Bates
Graham Nutbrown
Steve Skidmore
Christopher Stubbs

Oxford University Press

Contents

PART A Stories, poems and specials

Street games

Monsters, heroines, and villains

PART B Using words

Speaking and listening

Reading

Writing

Presentation

Punctuation:

Writing down speech:

Spelling:

4

Part A

Stories, poems and specials

Swap? sell? small ads sell fast

1950 Dad. Good runner; needs one or
Two repairs; a few grey hairs but
Nothing a respray couldn't fix
Would like a 1966 five-speed turbo
In exchange: something in the sporty
Twin-carb range.

1920s Granny. Not many like this
In such clean and rust-free state.
You must stop by to view! All chrome
As new, original fascia retained
Upholstery unstained. Passed MOT
Last week: will only swap for some-
Thing quite unique.

1986 low mileage Brother. As eco-
Nomical as any other. Must mention
Does need some attention. Stream-
Lined, rear spoiler. Runs on milk,
Baby oil and gripe water. Serviced;
Needs rear wash/wipe. Only one
Owner; not yet run in. Will swap
For anything.

Trevor Millum

On Tuesdays I polish my uncle

I went to play in the park.
I didn't get home until dark.
But when I got back I had ants in my pants,
And my father was feeding the shark.

I went to play in the park,
And I didn't come home until dark.
And when I got back I had ants in my pants,
And dirt in my shirt, and glue in my shoe,
And my father was tickling the shark.

I went to sleep in the park.
The shark was starting to bark.
And when I woke up I had ants in my pants,
Dirt in my shirt, glue in my shoe,
And beans in my jeans and a bee on my knee,
And the shark was tickling my father.

My father went off to the park.
I stayed home and read to the shark.
And when he got back he had ants in his pants,
Dirt in his shirt, glue in his shoe,
Beans in his jeans, a bee on his knee,
Beer in his ear and a bear in his hair,
So we put him outside in the ark.

I started the ark in the dark.
My father was parking the shark.
And when we got home we had ants in our pants,
Dirt in our shirt, glue in our shoe,
Beans in our jeans, a bee on our knee,
Beer in our ear and a bear in our hair,
A stinger in our finger, a stain in our brain,
And our belly-buttons shone in the dark.
So my dad he got snarky and barked at the shark,

Who was parking the ark on the mark in the dark.
And when they got back they had ants in their pants,
Dirt in their shirt, glue in their shoe,
Beans in their jeans, a bee on their knee,
Beer in their ear and a bear in their hair,
A stinger in each finger, a stain in the brain,
A small polka-dot burp, with headache tablets,
And a ship on the lip and a horse, of course,
So we all took a bath in the same tub and went to bed early.

Dennis Lee

Lost and found

I was worrying over some homework
When my Grandad walked into the room,
And sat wearily down with a grunt and a frown
And a face full of sorrow and gloom.

'I've lost it, I've lost it,' he muttered,
'And it's very important to me.'
'Lost what?' I replied. 'I've forgotten,' he sighed,
'But it's something beginning with T.'

'A toffee, perhaps,' I suggested,
'Or a teapot or even your tie,
Or some toast or a thread...' but he shook his grey head
As a tear trickled out of one eye.

'A tuba,' I said, 'or some treacle,
Or a toggle to sew on your mac,
Or a tray or a ticket, a tree or a thicket,
A thistle, a taper, a tack.'

But Grandad looked blank. 'Well, some tweezers,
Or a theory,' I said, 'or a tooth,
Or a tap or a till or a thought or a thrill,
Or your trousers, a trestle, the truth.'

'It's none of those things,' grumbled Grandad.
'A toy trumpet,' I offered, 'a towel,
Or a trout, a tureen, an antique tambourine,
A toboggan, a tortoise, a trowel...'

Then suddenly Grandad's scowl vanished,
'I've remembered!' he cried with a shout.
'It's my temper, you brat, so come here and take that!'
And he boxed both my ears and stalked out.

Richard Edwards

My hero

My dad's as brave as a dad can be,
I rate him Number One,
He's not afraid of the dead of night,
Or anything under the sun.

He's not afraid of a late-night film,
Full of horrors on the telly,
And is he afraid of skeletons?
Not dad, not on your Nelly!

He's not afraid of meeting ghosts,
He'd even smile and greet 'em,
And things that scare most dads the most,
My dad could just defeat 'em.

He's not afraid of vampires,
Or a wolf-man come to get him,
If Frankenstein's monster knocked on our door,
He wouldn't let that upset him.

My dad's as brave as a dad can be,
And he's always ready to prove it.
So why, when a spider's in the bath,
Does mum have to come and remove it?

Willis Hall

*A*untie

Up to the day she died, Auntie could thread the finest needle at one go. She did so on that last rainy day of her life. And, by the end of her life, her long sight had grown longer than anyone could possibly have expected.

Auntie's exceptional eyesight had been of no particular help to her in her job: she was a filing-clerk in a block of offices, for ever sorting other people's dull letters and dull memoranda. Boring; but Auntie was not ambitious, nor was she ever discontented.

Auntie's real interest – all her care – was for her family. She never married; but, by the time of her retirement from work, she was a great-aunt – although she was never called that – and she liked being one. She baby-sat, and took children to school, and helped with family expeditions. She knitted and crocheted and sewed – above all, she sewed. She mended and patched and made clothes.

She sewed by hand when necessary; otherwise she whirred the handle of an ancient sewing-machine, that had been a wedding-present to her mother long before.

Unfortunately, she was not particularly good at making clothes. Little Billy, her youngest great-nephew, was her last victim. 'Do I have to

wear this blazer-thing?' he whispered to his mother, Auntie's niece. (He whispered because – even in his bitterness – he did not want Auntie to overhear.) 'Honestly, Mum, no one at school ever wears anything looking like this.'

'Hush!' said his mother. Then: 'Auntie's very kind to take all that trouble, and to save us money, too. You should be grateful.'

'I'm not!' said little Billy, and he determined that when he was old enough, he wouldn't be at Auntie's mercy any more. Meanwhile, Auntie, who doted on Billy as the last child of his generation, was perplexed by the feeling that something she had done was not quite right.

Auntie was not a thinker, but she had common sense and – more and more – foresight. She knew, for instance, that nobody can live forever. One day she said: 'I wonder when I shall die? And how? Heart, probably. My old dad, your grandad, died of that.'

She was talking to the niece, Billy's mother, with whom Auntie now lived. The niece said: 'Oh, Auntie, don't talk so!'

Auntie said: 'My eyesight's as good as ever – well, better, really; but my hands aren't so much use.' She looked at her hands, knobbling with rheumatism. 'I can't use 'em as I once did.'

'Never mind!' said the niece.

'And the children are growing up. Even Billy.' Auntie sighed. 'Growing too old for me.'

'The children love their Auntie!' said the niece angrily.

This was true, in its way, but that did not prevent great-nephews and great-nieces becoming irritated when Auntie babied them and fussed over their clothing or over whatever they happened to be doing.

Auntie did not continue the argument with her niece. She was no good at discussion or argument anyway. That wasn't her strong point.

Her eyesight was her strong point, and yet also her worry. In old age she sat for long periods by her bedroom window, looking out over roof-tops to distant church spires and tower blocks. 'I don't like seeing so far,' she said once. 'What's the use to me? Or to anyone else?'

'You're lucky,' said her nephew-in-law, Billy's father. 'Some people would give their eyes to – well, they'd give a lot to have your eyesight at your age.'

'It's – it's wrong,' said Auntie, trying to explain something.

'If it happens that way, then it's natural,' said her nephew.

'Natural!' said Auntie; and she took to sitting at her bedroom window with her eyes closed.

One day: 'Asleep?' her niece asked softly.

'No.' Auntie's eyes opened at once. 'Just resting my eyes. Trying to get them not to go on with all this looking and looking, seeing and seeing...' Here Auntie paused, again attempting to sort out some ideas. But the ideas and what lay behind them could not be as easily sorted and filed into place as those documents in the office where she had worked years ago.

'Ah,' said the niece, preparing to leave it at that.

But Auntie had something more to say. 'When I'm in bed and asleep, I dream, and I know dreams are rubbish, so I needn't pay any attention to them. But when I sit here, wide awake, with my eyes open or even with my eyes closed, then...'

The niece waited.

Auntie said carefully: 'Then I think, and thinking must be like seeing: I see things.'

'What things?'

'Things a long way off.'

'That's because you're long-sighted, Auntie.'

'I wouldn't mind that. But the things a long way off are coming nearer.'

'Whatever do you mean?'

'How should I know what I mean? I'm just telling you what happens. I see things far away, and they're coming close. I don't understand it. I don't like it.'

'Perhaps you're just having day-dreams, Auntie.'

'You mean, it's all rubbish?'

'Well, is it?'

Auntie moved restlessly in her chair. She hated to be made to think in this way; but there were some things you had to think of with your mind, when you couldn't straightforwardly see them with your hands, to deal with them then and there.

There were these other things.

'No,' said Auntie crossly. 'They're not rubbish. All the same, I don't want to think about them. I don't want to talk about them.'

So there was no more talk about the far-away things that were coming nearer; but as for thinking – well, Auntie couldn't help doing that, in her way. Her life was uneventful, so that what she thought about naturally was what she saw with her eyes, or in her mind's eye.

One day the married niece asked if she could use Auntie's old sewing-machine to run up some curtains: her own machine had broken down.

'So has mine,' said Auntie. 'The needle's broken.'

'You have several spare needles, Auntie,' said the niece. 'I think I could put one in.'

The niece went downstairs to where the ancient sewing-machine was kept. When she had unlocked and taken off the wooden lid, she found that the needle was not broken, after all. It did not need replacing. She sighed to herself and smiled to herself at Auntie's mistake; and then she set to work with Auntie's sewing-machine.

She threaded up the machine with the right cotton for her curtains, arranged the material in the right position under the needle, and began to turn the handle of the machine. The stitching began; but the curtain material was very thick, and the needle penetrated it with difficulty...

With more difficulty at every stitch...

The needle broke.

So, after all, the niece had to change the needle, to finish machining her curtains. Later on, she said to Auntie: 'Your machine's all right now, but the needle broke.'

'I told you so,' said Auntie.

'No, Auntie. You said the needle had broken: you ought to have said, the needle will break.' The niece laughed jollily.

'I don't want to say things like that,' said Auntie. She spoke sharply, and her niece saw that she was upset for some reason.

So she said: 'Never mind, Auntie. It was just a funny thing to have happened, after what you said. A coincidence. Think no more of it.'

The niece thought no more of it; but Auntie did. She brooded over the strangeness of her long sight – over the seeing of far-away things that came nearer. She now kept that strangeness private to herself – secret; but sometimes something popped into a conversation before she could prevent it.

One family tea-time, when Auntie had been sitting silent for some time, she said: 'It's lucky there's never anyone left in those offices at night.'

'Which offices?'

'Where I used to work, of course.'

'Oh...' Nobody was interested, except for little Billy. He was always curious. 'Why is it lucky, Auntie?'

But already Auntie regretted having spoken; one could see that. 'No reason...' she said. 'Nothing... I was just thinking, that's all...'

The next morning, with Auntie's early cup of tea, the niece brought news.

'You'll never guess, Auntie!'

'Those old offices have burnt out.'

'Why, you have guessed! Yes, it was last night after you'd gone to bed early. An electrical short circuit started the fire, they think. Nobody's fault; and nobody hurt – nobody in the building.'

'No,' said Auntie. 'Nobody at all...'

'But you should have seen the blaze! You were asleep, so we didn't wake you; but we took little Billy to see. My goodness, Auntie! The smoke there was!'

'Yes,' said Auntie. 'the smoke...'

'And the flames – huge flames towering up!'

'Yes,' said Auntie. 'Five fire-engines...'

Her niece stared at her: 'There were five fire-engines; but how did you know?'

Auntie was flustered; and the niece went on staring. Auntie said: 'Well, a big blaze like that would need five fire-engines, wouldn't it?'

Her niece said nothing more; but, later, she reported the conversation to her husband. He was not impressed: 'Oh, I dare say she woke up and saw the fire through her bedroom window. With her long sight she saw the size of the fire, and – well, she realised it would need at least five fire-engines. As she said, more or less.'

'That's just possible as an explanation,' said his wife, 'if it weren't for one thing.'

'What thing?'

'Auntie's bedroom window doesn't look in that direction at all; her old office-block is on the other side of the house.'

'Oh!' said Auntie's nephew-in-law.

In the time that followed, Auntie was very careful indeed not to talk about her sight, long sight, or foresight. Even so, her niece sometimes watched her intently and oddly, as she sat by her bedroom window. And once her nephew-in-law sought her out to ask whether she would like to discuss with him the forthcoming Derby and which horse was likely to win the race. Auntie said she had never been interested in horse-racing, and disapproved of it because of the betting. So that was that.

One afternoon in early spring – not cold, but dreary and very overcast – Auntie was restless. She went downstairs to her sewing-machine and fiddled with it. She did a little hand-sewing on a pair of Billy's trousers, where a seam had come undone. (That was the last time she threaded a needle.)

Then she went upstairs, and came down again in her coat and hat.

'You're not thinking of going out, Auntie?' cried her niece. 'Today of all days? It's just beginning to rain!'

'A breath of fresh air, all the same,' said Auntie.

'It's not suitable for you, Auntie. So slippery underfoot on the pavements.'

Auntie said: 'I thought I'd go and meet Billy off the school bus.'

'Oh, Auntie! Billy's too old to need meeting off the bus nowadays. He doesn't need it, and he wouldn't like it. He'd hate it.'

Auntie sighed, hesitated, then slowly climbed up the stairs to her bedroom again.

Five minutes later she was coming downstairs again, almost hurriedly, still hatted and coated. She made for the stand where her umbrella was kept.

'Auntie!' protested the niece.

Auntie patted the handbag she was carrying: 'An important letter I've written, and must get into the post.'

Her niece gaped at her. Auntie never wrote important letters; she never wrote letters at all.

'About my pension,' Auntie explained. 'Private,' she added, as she saw that her niece was about to speak.

Her niece did speak, however. She had quite a lot to say. 'Auntie, your letter can't be all that urgent. And if it is, Billy will be home soon, and he'll pop to the pillar-box for you. It's really ridiculous – ridiculous – of you to think of going out in this wet, grey, slippery, miserable weather!'

Suddenly Auntie was different. She was resolved, stern in some strange determination. 'I must go,' she said, in such a way that her niece shrank back and let her pass.

So Auntie, her umbrella in one hand and her handbag in the other, set out.

The weather had worsened during the short delay. She had to put up her umbrella at once against the rain. She hurried along towards the

pillar-box – hurried, but with care, because the pavement and road surfaces were slippery, just as her niece had said.

The pillar-box lay a very little way beyond the bus-stop where Billy's school bus would arrive. There was a constant to and fro of traffic, but no bus was in sight. Instead of going on to the pillar-box, Auntie hesitated a moment, then took shelter from the rain in the doorway of a gent's outfitter's, just by the bus-stop. From inside the shop, an assistant, as he said later, observed the old lady taking shelter, and observed all that happened afterwards.

Auntie let down her umbrella, furled it properly, and held it in her right hand, her handbag in her left.

The shop assistant, staring idly through his shop-window, saw the school bus approaching its stop, through almost blinding rain.

The old lady remained in the doorway.

The school bus stopped. The children began to get off. The traffic swirled by on the splashing road.

The old lady remained in the doorway.

The shop assistant's attention was suddenly caught by something happening out on the road, in the passing traffic. A car had gone out of control on the slippery road. It was swerving violently; it narrowly missed another car, and began skidding across the road, across the back of the school bus. Nearly all the children were away from the bus by now – except for one, slower than the rest. In a moment of horror, the shop assistant saw him, unforgettably: a little boy, wearing a badly-made blazer, who was going to be run over and killed.

The assistant gave a cry and ran to the door, although he knew he would be too late.

But someone else was ahead of him, from that same doorway. The old lady darted – no, flung herself – flew – forwards towards the child.

There were two – perhaps three – seconds for action before the car would hit the child. The old lady wouldn't reach him in that time; but the assistant saw her swing her right arm forward, the hand clutching a furled umbrella by its ferrule. The crook of the umbrella hooked inside the front of the little boy's blazer and hooked him like a fish from water out of the path of the skidding car.

The old lady fell over backwards on the pavement, with the child on top of her, and the car skidded past them, crashed into the bus-stop itself, and stopped. The driver sat stupefied inside, white-faced, shocked, but otherwise uninjured.

Nobody was injured, except Auntie. She died in the ambulance, on her way to the hospital. Heart, the doctors said. No wonder, at her age, and in such extraordinary circumstances.

Much later, after the funeral, Billy's mother looked for the letter that Auntie had written to the pension people. 'It should have been in her handbag, because the shopman said she didn't go on to the pillar-box to post anything. But it wasn't in her handbag.'

'She must have left it behind by mistake,' said Billy's father. 'All that pension business ceases with her death.'

'I don't want the letter,' said his wife. 'I just want to know whether there ever was one.'

'What are you driving at?'

'Don't you see? The letter was an excuse.'

'An excuse?'

'She wanted an excuse to be at that bus-stop when Billy got off, because she knew what was going to happen. She foresaw.'

They stared at each other. Then the nephew said: 'Second sight – that's what you mean, isn't it? But it's one thing to foresee, say, which horse is going to win the Derby. And it's quite another thing to foresee what's going to happen, and then deliberately to prevent its happening. That's altering the course of things... That's altering everything...'

The niece said: 'But you don't understand. She foresaw that Billy would be in danger of being killed, so she went to save him. But she also foresaw that very thing – I mean, she foresaw that she would go to save him. That she would save him. Although it killed her.'

The nephew liked a logical argument, even about illogical things. He said: 'She could still have altered that last part of what she foresaw. She

16

could have decided not to go to the bus-stop, because she foresaw that it would all end in her death. After all, nobody wants to die.'

'You still don't understand,' his wife said. 'You don't understand Auntie. She knew she would save Billy, even if she had to die for it. She had to do it, because it was her nature to do it. Because she was Auntie. Don't you see?'

The nephew, seeing something about Auntie he had never properly perceived before, said quite humbly: 'Yes, I see...'

And the niece, leaning on his shoulder, wept again for Auntie, whom she had known so well since she had been a very little girl. Known so well, perhaps, that she had not known Auntie truly for what she really was, until then.

As for Billy, he never said much about that rainy day, the last of Auntie's life. He hadn't gone to Auntie's funeral – children often don't. But he wore his horrible home-made blazer until he grew out of it. And he never, never forgot Auntie.

Philippa Pearce

Swap? sell? small ads sell fast

Writing

This poem is funny because it treats people as if they were second-hand cars for sale. Try writing your own 'Ads' for people you know:

- second-hand car ads for friends at school – or other members of the family
- advertising members of the family as if they were houses for sale
- advertising lessons at school as if they were TV programmes

---

On Tuesdays I polish my uncle

A group reading

There is only one thing to do with this crazy poem – and that's to read it aloud. But how ?

1 On your own read the poem and think about how it should be read by the group.
2 Discuss how to divide it. Remember that any part of the poem can be read by one person, or two – or by the whole group. Try to work out a pattern that is varied and fun
3 When you have decided who will read what, practise your reading. You will probably need several practices.

Lost and found

Writing

Part of the fun of the poem is all the crazy things that 'I' suggests Grandad may have lost.

1 Make a list of all the unlikely things you can think of, beginning with 'T', that Grandad may have lost. (You may find a dictionary helpful here.)
2 Look through your list for words that rhyme.
3 Write a verse for the poem that uses some of your words. Remember that it rhymes in two places:

'A tuba,' I said, 'or some treacle,
Or a toggle to sew on your *mac*,
Or a tray or a **ticket**, a tree or a **thicket**,
A thistle, a taper, a *tack*.'

4 Write your own *Lost and found* poem, using a different letter. For example you could use the letter P, in which case the last two lines might be:

'It's my patience, you brat, so come here and take that!'
And he boxed both my ears and stalked out.

Auntie

Thinking about the story

1 Where do we first learn about Auntie's excellent eye-sight ?
2 Where do we first learn that Auntie can see into the future ?
3 How do we know that Auntie did not see the fire at the office block where she used to work ?
4 What exactly did Auntie foresee on the last afternoon of her life ?
5 Why did Auntie save Billy's life, even though she knew that she herself would die ?

Auntie's character

Think about what Auntie was like as a person. You may find it helpful to make a chart about her like the one below.

Now write as much as you can about Auntie – the sort of person she was, what members of her family thought of her, what her niece realises about her at the end. What do you think of her ?

Writing : an ordinary person ?

Auntie is ordinary in nearly every way, but she had one very special quality. Try writing your own story about a person who is ordinary except for one special quality.
Here are some examples:

- they can see in the dark
- they can never ever tell a lie
- when they are with other people they know what they are thinking
- they are living backwards in time – they were born in the future and so instead of getting older, they get younger. (And instead of remembering the past, they are forgetting the future...?)

Auntie's special qualities	Auntie's weaker points

This is a story about the Greek hero Theseus.

Theseus hurried back to tell his father what he had decided.

A

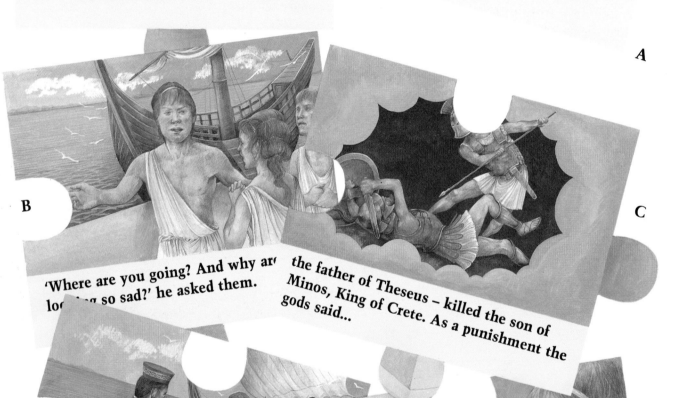

B

C

'Where are you going? And why are looking so sad?' he asked them.

the father of Theseus – killed the son of Minos, King of Crete. As a punishment the gods said...

D

'Go if you must,' he said, 'but when you return, put red sails on your ship. If I see it has black sails, I shall know you are dead.'

E

They told him they were being taken to Crete, where they would be sacrificed to...

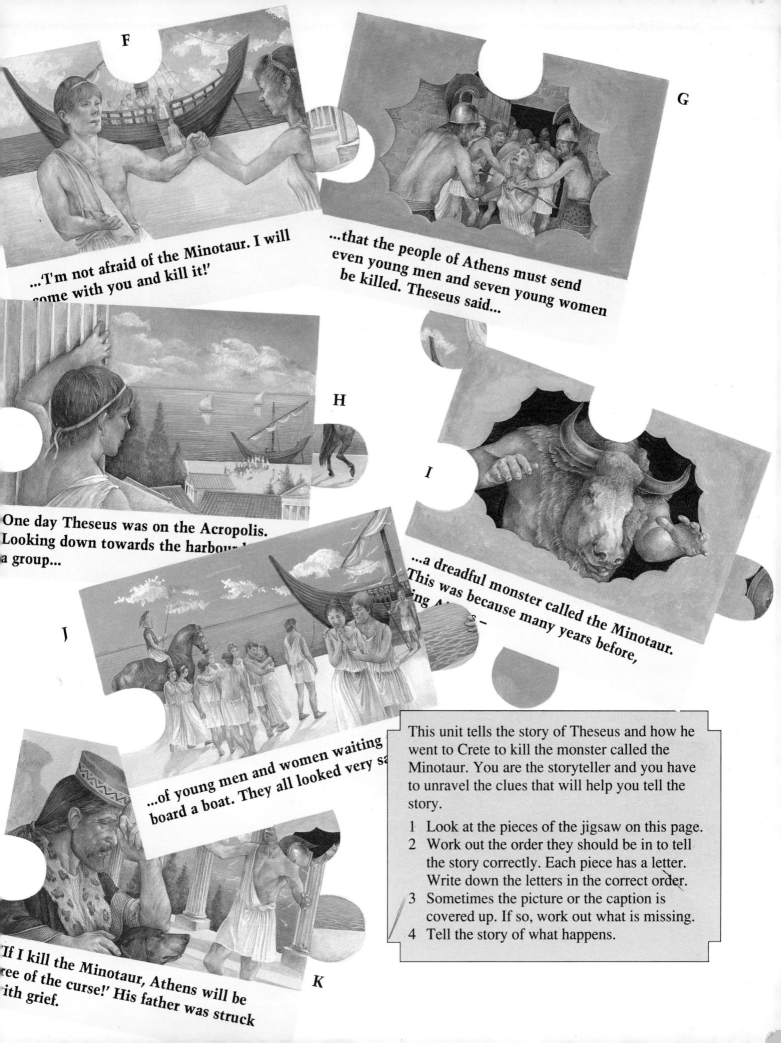

F ...'I'm not afraid of the Minotaur. I will come with you and kill it!'

G ...that the people of Athens must send even young men and seven young women be killed. Theseus said...

H One day Theseus was on the Acropolis. Looking down towards the harbour... a group...

I ...a dreadful monster called the Minotaur. This was because many years before,

J ...of young men and women waiting board a boat. They all looked very sa

K 'If I kill the Minotaur, Athens will be ree of the curse!' His father was struck ith grief.

This unit tells the story of Theseus and how he went to Crete to kill the monster called the Minotaur. You are the storyteller and you have to unravel the clues that will help you tell the story.

1 Look at the pieces of the jigsaw on this page.
2 Work out the order they should be in to tell the story correctly. Each piece has a letter. Write down the letters in the correct order.
3 Sometimes the picture or the caption is covered up. If so, work out what is missing.
4 Tell the story of what happens.

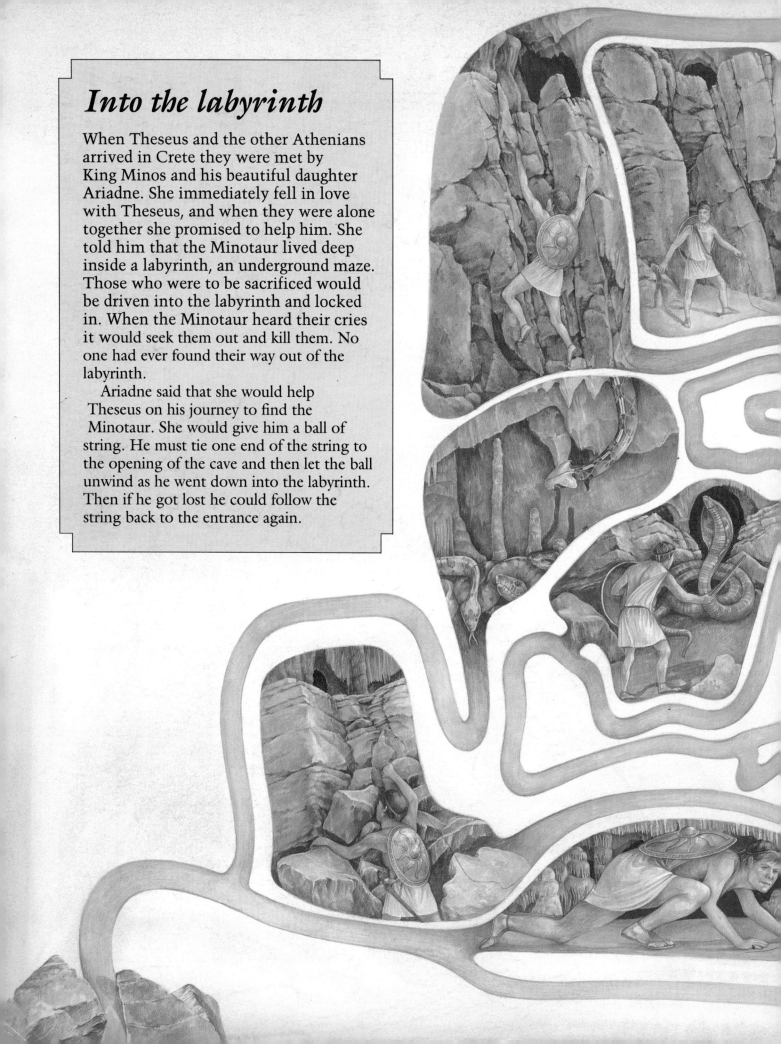

Into the labyrinth

When Theseus and the other Athenians arrived in Crete they were met by King Minos and his beautiful daughter Ariadne. She immediately fell in love with Theseus, and when they were alone together she promised to help him. She told him that the Minotaur lived deep inside a labyrinth, an underground maze. Those who were to be sacrificed would be driven into the labyrinth and locked in. When the Minotaur heard their cries it would seek them out and kill them. No one had ever found their way out of the labyrinth.

Ariadne said that she would help Theseus on his journey to find the Minotaur. She would give him a ball of string. He must tie one end of the string to the opening of the cave and then let the ball unwind as he went down into the labyrinth. Then if he got lost he could follow the string back to the entrance again.

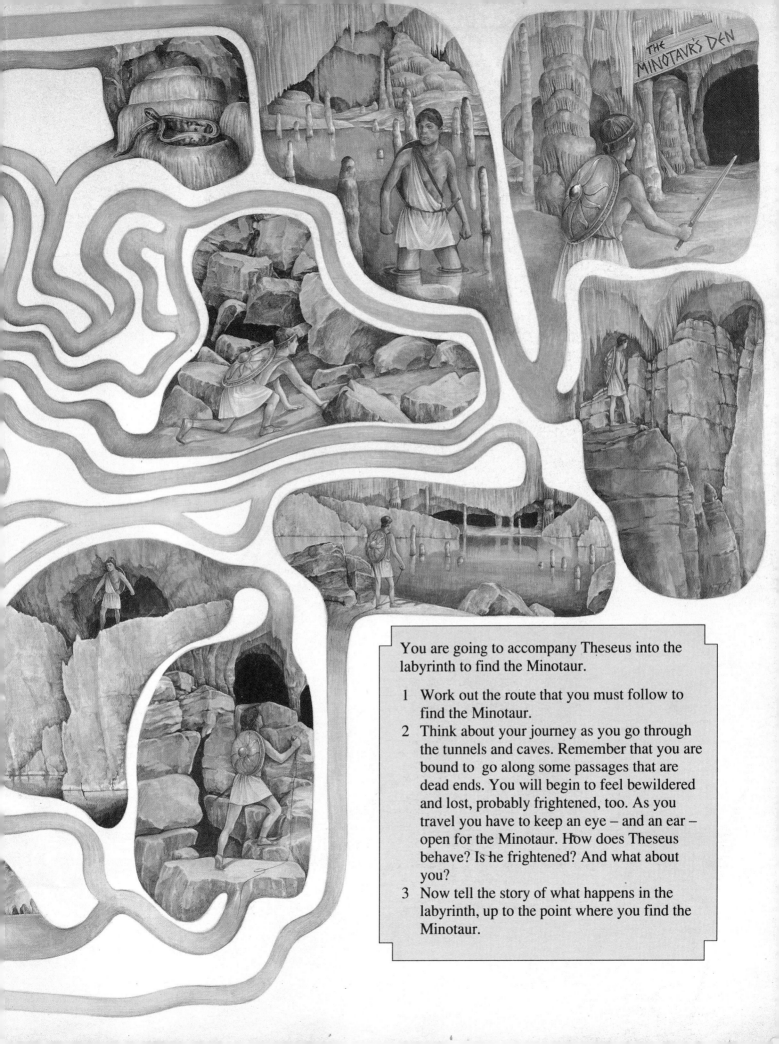

You are going to accompany Theseus into the labyrinth to find the Minotaur.

1   Work out the route that you must follow to find the Minotaur.
2   Think about your journey as you go through the tunnels and caves. Remember that you are bound to go along some passages that are dead ends. You will begin to feel bewildered and lost, probably frightened, too. As you travel you have to keep an eye – and an ear – open for the Minotaur. How does Theseus behave? Is he frightened? And what about you?
3   Now tell the story of what happens in the labyrinth, up to the point where you find the Minotaur.

THE MINOTAUR'S DEN

The Minotaur

Now it is time to fight the Minotaur!
Look at the picture and imagine what happened
in the fight. Work out the answers to these
questions.

How did it start?
Who made the first move?
How did the Minotaur move and fight?
How did Theseus move and fight?
What sounds could be heard?

What could you smell and taste during the fight?
What did you feel?
What were the colours and patterns?
How long did it go on?
Were you frightened for Theseus at any stage?
How did it end?
What state was Theseus in at the end?

Now tell the story.

25

Escape

Theseus made his way back through the labyrinth and out into the fresh night air where Ariadne was waiting for him. Now they had to rescue the Athenians and make their escape. There was still much danger: the palace was heavily guarded, and even if they got away King Minos had many warships which could chase and sink them.

Use the words and pictures on these pages to help you build up a picture of what happened. Work out the answers to these questions:

Where were the Athenians held captive?
Where were the guards?
What was the best route in and out of the palace?
How did they get from the palace to the ships?
How could they stop the warships from chasing them?
What mistake did they make as they sailed away?
What do you think happened in the end?

Now tell the story of the escape.

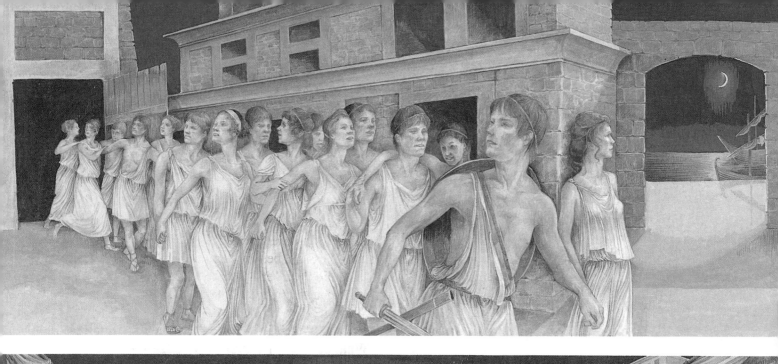

First night in Apton Magna

That first night in Apton Magna I had a dream. You know what it's like when you move house. We'd driven all the way from Bedford to Yorkshire and then spent six hours lugging furniture and other junk around. It was a Sunday — what Dad calls the day of rest, which is a bit of a laugh, considering. By nine o'clock I was shattered. They'd bought this enormous house, Four Winds, which used to be the local manor or something. It had six bedrooms, which works out at two each, as well as two bathrooms and about eight downstairs rooms. I don't know why we needed a place that size. When I asked Dad he mumbled something about entertaining so maybe he was planning to turn it into a theatre or something. It was like three ants moving into Wembley Stadium.

Anyway, I was shattered and I went to bed. I had to go up this wide, curving staircase and along about three miles of landing to get to my room. It was a big, square room with a polished floor and a high ceiling. There was no carpet, and my single bed and bits of furniture looked lost in it. It reminded me of those rooms they put guests in in horror movies — the sort where you know something horrible's going to happen in the middle of the night. Maybe that's what brought the dream on.

It was a weird dream — more of a nightmare, really. It was dark and I was walking along an unmade road alone. I was coming into Apton Magna though it didn't look anything like Apton Magna. There was just a rough road with little houses on either side, and what looked like a church on a low hill. I think I'd been expecting something good when I reached the village — a bed for the night, perhaps — but the place was deserted. Doors stood half open and the wind whined through black, unglazed windows. A feeling of dread gripped me and I started to run. There was something lying on the ground in front of me and I tried to jump over it, but my feet wouldn't leave the ground and I sort of waded through it. It was a bundle of rags that was hard inside. There was a scraping, rattling sound and when I looked down I saw bones. I screamed. The scream woke me, and I lay in a cold sweat with a voice in my head saying, 'Hidden, but here forever.'

The scream must have been real, because Mum came in and put the light on. I told her I'd been dreaming and she sat on the bed and held my hand for a bit. I've had bad dreams since I was very small and she's used to it. 'It's the move,' she murmured. 'Finding yourself in a strange room. It's all over now.'

It wasn't, though. I knew, and so did she. It never is when I dream.

Robert Swindells

Mrs Sugar

I know this is a true story, because when my Aunt Peg was a little girl she used to live next door to Mrs Sugar, who was a witch. Mrs Sugar used to curl her hair with rags and take snuff, and every Saturday she had a bet on the horses. Everybody in the street knew she was a witch. She used to give you silverweed for freckles and camomile for belly-ache.

Anyway, Mrs Sugar died, and she was buried in the cemetery, and had an angel on her grave. Soon after a story started going round that Mrs Sugar was still taking her usual walk out on Saturday evenings. I don't know how the story got started. Maybe people thought that since she'd been a witch when alive, she'd be a ghost once she was dead.

Most adults said the story was just a story, but most children believed it, and they used to go in gangs to the cemetery, especially on a Saturday night, and peer through the railings, trying to spot Mrs Sugar coming out. If a cat stuck its leg in the air, they all raced off, screaming that they'd seen something move. A lot of them said they'd seen Mrs Sugar, but none of them really had, and nobody believed them.

After weeks of this game, they got bored with Mrs Sugar, since she never turned up, no matter how long they watched for her. In fact, when my Aunt Peg got the idea to scare her friends, she'd forgotten all about Mrs Sugar. It was Hallowe'en coming up that gave her the idea – they'd had lessons at school about ghosts, witches and Hallowe'en. The teachers said that ghosts looked like people with bed-sheets over their heads, and that witches all had cats and flew about on broomsticks. They never said anything about snuff, silverweed and horse-racing. So Peg never gave Mrs Sugar a thought.

What Peg did was to take a bed-sheet from home and sneak off with it. That wasn't hard, because her mother worked at night, and Peg could do as she liked. She and all her friends used to run the streets till all hours, and she knew that her friends would come looking for her. They'd search the glass-tip, the marl-hole, the brickyard, and they'd go up and down the canal tow-path, looking under the bridges. She had only to hide at one of these places and wait, and they would all come along sooner or later. Then she'd jump out and scare them to death!

The tow-path was nearest, so she went there, and she crouched down under the hedge, amongst all the long grasses and bushes. She pulled the sheet half over her head, to be ready to jump out, and she waited.

She knew that it was going to seem like forever, waiting for her friends, because the time you spend waiting always seems longer than it really is. So she was patient, and even when she was fed up she stuck it out. She didn't realise how dark it was getting, because she was by the canal, and it's always lighter by water than it is anywhere else. Then she heard someone come through the bushes behind her – 'Oh damn!' she thought: her friends had found her. She turned round, but the sheet flopped over her face and she couldn't see anything but white.

Whoever it was stood close beside her in the grass, and said, 'Hello, Peggie.'

Peg pulled the sheet away from her face, and saw an old pair of battered old button-up boots. The voice above her said, 'You're here to frighten, Peggie?'

Peg looked up, and saw Mrs Sugar.

Mrs Sugar bent down and looked close into Peg's face. 'And I'm here to frighten – let's frighten together!'

It was a week before Peg's heart slowed down. Nobody would believe her when she told them she'd seen Mrs Sugar. 'That old story,' they said.

I believed her, when she told me, when she was my Auntie Peg. 'Don't believe books,' she told me. 'Them teachers get stuff out of books. But witches don't have pointed hats, and ghosts don't look like sheets. I know they don't, because I saw Mrs Sugar.'

Susan Price

How to be a ghost

Have you ever thought seriously about what it's like to be a ghost? I bet you haven't, any more than I did. While you're still a lifer you're generally more interested in what it would be like to see a ghost. You never think what it's like to be one of us. So now I'm going to tell you.

First of all, there aren't all that many of us who want to come back haunting after we're dead. Most of us are quite pleased not to have to bother about it. We mostly want to be left to get on with Afterwards. And I'm not going to tell you what Afterwards is like. You wouldn't understand, and, anyway, I'm not supposed to try.

The ghosts who do want to go haunting, do it for all sorts of different reasons. Some of them just want to go back to places they liked while they were still alive. Sometimes it's so they can moon around and say how beautiful it all was and pretend they're still lifers there. Sometimes they think they want to see how it looks now. That can be very disappointing, especially if they leave it too long. I've known ghosts who went back to their houses or caravans or their stately homes and there wasn't a trace of them left, it was all tower blocks or allotments or – one lady ghost told me – a supermarket. That particular ghost was sad at first, because she'd lived in a hulking great castle with fields and

forests and things, and when she saw it again it was a council estate and, as I said, a supermarket. But she loved it, after a time. She said how convenient it would have been for her, instead of having to wait for chaps to go out and kill rabbits and deer and all that, and for the peasants to bring in the vegetables; she'd much rather have been able just to nip down to the shops and buy what she needed, when she needed it. 'You can't think what a lot went to waste before they invented fridges,' she told me.

That reminds me of the ghosts who really want to know what's going on. They don't haunt because they want to wring their hands and wail about something that happened hundreds of years ago. They want to know about the latest inventions. Sometimes they come back from their haunts very cross, and say, 'If only I'd known about that,' or 'Why didn't I think of that?' But generally they enjoy themselves and they play around with inventions and machines like nobody's business. Of course that isn't really allowed, but once you've got back as a ghost, there's not much anybody can do to stop you. There was a poet I met, quite young, who hadn't ever got his poems published while he was alive, so when he discovered a computer in the office where he'd worked, he fed all sorts of things into it which weren't supposed to be there. When the office lifers came the next day and tried to make the computer come up with some figures they wanted, what it printed out was this poet's poetry instead. He told me they were very cross and they started saying there must be a ghost in the machine. He wasn't a very good poet, I don't think, but it was nice for him to see his poems printed for once. Even if he was dead first.

The sort of ghost everyone knows about is the sort who goes haunting because he's trying to get a lifer to do something for him, like revenge his horrible murder, or discover the hidden treasure, or find a will that's been lost. Those ghosts are mostly angry; they are also what I call the show-off ghosts. They love dressing up. They wear clanking armour, or white sheets with skulls, or black velvet and white ruffs like Mary Queen of Scots.

Often those aren't at all the sort of clothes they wore while they were alive, but they think it makes them grander when they start saying 'REVENGE ME!' or 'OH HORROR, HORROR!' and things like that.

They act a lot; sometimes I see them practising in front of mirrors, making faces and trying out their voices. What's really annoying for them is when the lifers they're visiting can't see them or hear them either. I suppose you do know that not everyone can see ghosts or hear them or even feel them. Kids are good at it. I've never not been seen by a kid. But for the dressing-up ghosts it just about sends them crazy, after all that bother, finding the right clothes, and often arranging to carry their heads in funny places – I mean not on their necks – and then the lifer just doesn't take any notice. Hamlet's father's ghost was lucky; at least Hamlet saw him, even if some of the others didn't. I can tell you, a great many ghosts go to a lot of trouble, and don't get any thanks for it. It's an unjust world.

There are rules we have to keep. I suppose everyone has to keep to some sort of rule. There isn't anything we can't go through – stone, brick, concrete, wood, plastic – you name it, we can get through. I don't like plastic much; it's somehow a bit sticky, it sort of clings. And we can appear and disappear just when we like, which can be very convenient. But we can't haunt places we'd never been to, which is a bore for me, because I was so young when I died I'd hardly been anywhere. I'd have liked to see some of the famous places, like Rome and Paris and Moscow and South Sea islands and Jamaica and New York. But when you're a kid of ten you don't get to see places like that, so I never will. As a matter of fact I don't haunt much. I did just at first, because I missed my Mum, so I used to go back to visit her. But she couldn't ever see me, though I think at first she knew I was around, so now I mostly stay where I am and amuse myself with some of the other kids who are here too. Sometimes I'm sent on what's called 'duty'. That's for things like looking after babies who've been left alone too long, or playing with little kids who get lonely. I had one really nice job, playing with a kid called Mike. We used to build Lego together and make up stories about the fellows who lived in the Lego houses, and if Mike talked about me, people just thought he was making me up. But then one day, I went to visit Mike, and he couldn't see me. He couldn't hear me, either. I was quite upset. Then I saw that he'd got too old. He was like the rest of the lifers, he didn't need me any more. But it was a pity, I'd really liked playing with Mike.

Sometimes we get sent to fetch lifers to come over to our side. Kids get used for this quite a lot, because it isn't as frightening for the lifers to be fetched by a kid. And we're given a bit of time. You don't just walk up to someone and say, 'Hi! You're going to die, I've come to fetch you.' You have time to let them get used to you. All the same, it's not a job I fancy. I like it better when I'm sent to look after a baby or play with a kid like Mike.

That's about all I can tell you. I don't know why anyone hasn't thought of saying it all before. Not that there's anything new to say now. Haunting has been going on for years and years and years. I just thought you might like to have an up-to-date report. That's all.

Catherine Storr

At nine of the night I opened my door

At nine of the night I opened my door
That stands midway between moor and moor,
And all around me, silver-bright,
I saw that the world had turned to white.

Thick was the snow on field and hedge
And vanished was the river's edge,
Where winter skilfully had wound
A shining scarf without a sound.

And as I stood and gazed my fill
A stable-boy came down the hill.
With every step I saw him take
Flew at his heel a puff of flake.

His brow was whiter than the hoar,
A beard of freshest snow he wore,
And round about him, snow-flake starred,
A red horse-blanket from the yard.

In a red cloak I saw him go,
His back was bent, his step was slow,
And as he laboured through the cold
He seemed a hundred winters old.

I stood and watched the snowy head,
The whiskers white, the cloak of red.
'A Merry Christmas!' I heard him cry.
'The same to you, old friend,' said I.

Charles Causley

A story about death

It was a Tuesday morning in spring when Death walked in our kitchen door. Mama was taking cookies out of the oven. I was sitting on the floor of the pantry, in my special place, drawing and feeling a little sad. Mama was annoyed with me for leaving my baby brother asleep on the big bed in the playroom. He was lying in the middle of the bed with our stuffed animals around him and a big pile of clean laundry at the foot of the bed. He couldn't roll off, but Mama says we might forget he is there in the middle of that mess, and do a somersault on him. True, my sister and I usually do somersaults on that bed.

Death didn't even knock. The door opened and I smelled a basement smell and felt cold air all around me. He didn't see me. He just looked at the cookies on the table and at the cake Mama had just frosted. He looked and looked at that cake. I looked and looked at him. He was just like the pictures of him in books: yellowish-white bones in a long brown robe. The hood was pulled up so that you could hardly see his head. He looked up from the cake at Mama.

'I've come for one of your children. You have three.' He held up his bony fingers and counted, 'One seven-year-old, one five-year-old, and one baby two months old. Which will it be?'

Mama stopped taking cookies off the baking-sheet. She didn't even look scared. 'Must it be one of the children? How about me?'

'How about me!' mimicked Death in a high, mean voice. 'Aw. You parents are all the same. No. I have my orders. It must be a child, by twelve noon, so make up your mind. I'm late.'

Mama didn't answer him. Was she mad enough to give me to him? I wanted to run to her, but I stayed very still, like a little animal in the forest. I made myself as small as I could and waited to hear what Mama would say. But Mama still didn't answer, just poured a mug of tea for Death, then took a sip of her tea. Death ate six cookies in a flash. I have never seen anyone so greedy. Mama poured some milk into her tea. She drank slowly, with a serious face. I could hardly sit still. Death helped himself to another six cookies.

The kitchen clock hummed. Death crunched his cookies and slurped his tea. Finally Mama said, very slowly, with sips of tea in between, 'I have read somewhere that you like games.'

'No. No. No games. Those days are over.'

'And must it be today?' continued Mama, as if Death had not interrupted her.

'Well,' said Death, with a mouth full of cookie, 'I must do my job by noon.'

Mama got a big knife and cut a large slice of cake, put it on a plate, and got out a fork. Then she offered the plate of cake to Death.

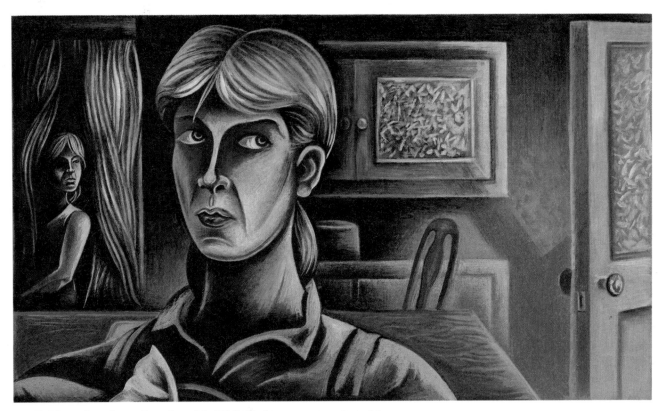

Taking the plate, Death said, 'If I don't get one today, I have two more chances.'

Mama looked interested. 'The children are so young. If you don't get one now, then all of them get to grow very old, to be truly ready for you?'

'Well, yes. I get three tries this time. But I won't miss. No tricks. I'm watching the clock. Well. Which one?' He mumbled because his mouth was full of cake.

Mama took a deep breath. 'I'm thinking.'

The clock said one minute to twelve.

'Hurry, woman!' gasped Death, nearly choking on his cake. The plate clattered to the kitchen table. As he stood up, all kinds of crumbs fell from his robe to the kitchen floor.

'I suppose it must be the baby,' whispered Mama. Her back was to me and I saw that she had her fingers crossed behind her back as she spoke. I nearly cried out.

Death raced upstairs. 'He's not in his bed!' he yelled.

'Oh,' said Mama. 'Where can he be?'

She looked at me and put her finger to her lips, then got out the broom and began to sweep up the crumbs.

Death raced downstairs and out the front door to look in the baby carriage under the cherry tree. It was empty. Then he looked in the baby's bouncy chair.

Twelve was striking on the church clock. I counted under my breath. Eleven. Twelve.

Death slammed out of the kitchen door. 'I'll be back tomorrow,' he called over his shoulder, and was gone.

Mama and I raced upstairs. The baby was safe, asleep under a large fuzzy bear, the one I've slept with since I was two.

'Mama, what will you do?' I asked.

Mama gave me a big hug. 'I'm thinking. With the baby it may just be possible to trick him two more times.'

All afternoon Mama was very quiet. She made me promise not to tell what had happened. 'I'm not sure that we can trust Death, so be very quiet, and I'll think.'

I begged not to go to school the next day, but Mama said that I was over my cold and that I would be safer at school in case her trick should fail.

That night when dinner was over, Mama left us reading with Papa and went out. She came back later with a shopping bag full of something that looked like boxes. We asked if she had been shopping, and she said no, she had been to friends borrowing.

Late that night, I thought I heard the baby crying, but when I got up to look, he was quietly asleep in his bed.

Mama made me go to school, but I crept back home just before noon. Death was there, in the kitchen. The whole house smelled delicious. Mama had made a big kettle of soup. Death was just finishing a bowl of it.

'I was angry with you yesterday,' he said, 'but you are a wonderful cook.' He held out his bowl for a second helping, then ate it rapidly, spilling some on his robe. 'However,' he continued between spoonfuls, 'you must learn to accept things.'

He held out his bowl for another helping. 'Who would leave a baby on a bed full of stuffed animals and clean laundry anyway? He might fall off!' He put down his spoon. 'I hear the baby crying now. I'll just go get him.'

Mama looked stern. 'It is rude to ask for thirds and not to finish.'

Death finished his soup quickly and headed out of the kitchen door. The crying came from the study. Death ran in. No baby, just a tape recorder playing a tape of my little sister crying when she was a baby.

Then we heard another cry. 'Wa-a-a-a! Wa-a-a-a!' Death raced up to the baby's bed. Another tape recorder. 'Not here!' yelled Death. 'Wait. I'll smell him out.' But when he sniffed the whole house was full of the smell of the soup. 'Wa-a-a-a,' came another long cry from the guest bedroom. But there was another tape recorder. In every room a tape recorder played the calls and cries of babies. Death raced from room to room, his robe flapping. His voice was angrier and angrier. My heart was pounding as I began to count the strokes of the church clock. I could hardly hear it for all of the babies crying... six... seven... eight... nine... ten... eleven... twelve.

'You think you're so smart,' Death snarled at Mama. 'Tomorrow I won't miss.'

He slammed the back door. Mama went through the house turning off recorders. Just then the baby awoke and began to call. 'Aya, aya, aya.' I ran to the pantry. My baby brother was on top of the refrigerator on a

bed of clean nappies and towels in his plastic baby bath-tub.

As Mama fed the baby, she began to cry. She didn't even scold me for coming home to spy.

'Mama, what will you do now?' I asked as I stroked the baby's fuzzy head. He stopped eating to grin at me. He has no teeth, so it is all gums and drool when he smiles.

'He has only one more try,' said Mama.

The next day I had just managed to sneak home and hide when Death arrived. He was early. Mama was holding the baby in her arms when Death walked in the door. On the kitchen table were three loaves of freshly-baked bread, a full butter dish and a big bread knife. On the sideboard was a large fat hen Mama was planning to roast for dinner.

Death helped himself to bread and butter. 'I'm glad you are going to be reasonable,' he said.

'May I just feed him first?' asked Mama softly.

My baby brother gurgled and cooed in her arms. Then he began to chew his fist. 'Oh. All right, but no more delay. I can't stand about nattering all day with you. I have work to do,' Death complained. He cut another slice of bread and spread the butter on it from edge to edge very carefully before he took a big bite.

Mama wrapped the baby in a big blue flannel blanket and sat down in the kitchen armchair to nurse. Death poured himself a mug of tea and took another slice of bread and butter.

It was nearly twelve when Mama began to burp the baby. The telephone rang. 'Answer that, will you please?' Mama said to Death.

Death went to the telephone in the front hall.

The baby burped a big one.

Death held the receiver against his chest and leaned around the kitchen door. 'It's a carpet-cleaning service. They have a special on this week. Do you want the carpets cleaned?'

'No, thank you,' said Mama, as she put the baby to the other breast.

The church clock began to strike twelve. Death slammed down the telephone and ran into the kitchen. 'No more fooling!' he said as he snatched the bundle from Mama's arms and rushed out the back door. Mama hid her face in her hands.

The clock was silent. Then we heard Death's angry wail 'Cheat! Che-e-e-eat!' he cried. But he didn't come back.

Mama looked up and gave a great big sigh. 'He's gone.'

Very slowly she leaned over to reach under the table. She lifted the towel that covered the big bowl we use for making bread. There was my baby brother, chewing on his fist. I couldn't believe my eyes.

'Mama. I didn't see you do that,' I said.

Mama pointed to the sideboard, and then picked up my baby brother. I looked to where she pointed and began to laugh and jump up and down. The fat hen was gone.

'Yug-g-g, Mama,' I said. 'You held that cold thing to your breast!'

Judith Gorog

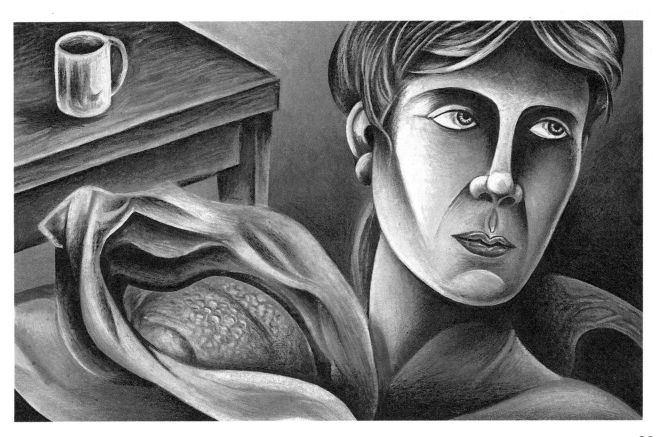

Ghost stories

Working on your own

1 How many ghost stories can you think of ?
2 Do you believe in ghosts ?
3 Do you know anybody who has ever seen a ghost ?
4 Think of one ghost story that you can remember – or make one up. Think of all the details.

Working with a partner

Take it in turns to tell your stories to each other. When you have both finished, talk about them and think of ways in which each of them could be improved.

On your own

Now write your ghost story and remember to include all the improvements you thought of when you were talking to your partner.

Groups of 4 or 5

1 Pass round all the stories so that everyone has a chance to read them all.
2 Choose one of the stories to work on. Either have one person reading the story, or have different people reading different parts. Illustrate the story with ghostly sound effects. You can either perform the story live or record it on a cassette-recorder.
3 Discuss all these points. Decide:
   ● how the story will be read and who will read it
   ● what sound effects you need
   ● how they will be made and who will make them.
4 Now practise your reading until you are satisfied that it is the best you can do.

First night in Apton Magna

1 So what do you think happened ?
2 This passage comes from the beginning of a long story. Does it give you any clues about what happened later ?
3 Make a list of any clues you can find and beside each one say what it suggests to you about what will happen later in the story.
4 Make up a continuation of the story, using any clues you can find.

Mrs Sugar

1 What impression did you get of the place where the story is set ?
2 How did the life of the children at that time compare with your life ?
3 Do you believe in ghosts ? How does this affect what you think of the story ?

Writing

'Nobody would believe her when she told them she'd seen Mrs Sugar.' How do you think the conversation went ? (Remember that 'It was a week before Peg's heart slowed down.') Write the conversation in which Peg tells her friends what happened to her and how she felt about it.

How to be a ghost

Here are some ideas for following up the advice
in **How to be a ghost...**

Guidelines for Ghosts
A brochure introducing
Afterwards to newcomers
and setting out some do's
and don'ts.

The Ghostly Code
A short version for ghosts who
aren't very good at reading - or
can't be bothered !
The first part of the set could be
based on the rules you learn from
the story.
The second part could be based on
the rules you are able to invent.

Haunting Party
An advertisement in the
Afterwards Advertiser for
ghosts who might like to
join a haunting group.

At nine of the night

This poem describes something that happened to the poet.

1 When did it happen ?
2 What did he actually see ?
3 What did it make him think of ?
4 What made him think like that ?

A story about death

Characters

This story is like a battle between the
storyteller's mother and Death. As we read it we
get a good idea of the character of each one.
What impression did you get of the mother ?
And of Death ?

1 Choose words and phrases to describe each of
   them. You can choose from the list opposite,
   but try to think of your own words too. Not
   all the words are suitable, so do not feel that
   you must use all of them.

affectionate	imaginative
bad tempered	mean
calm	sly
clever	spiteful
easily fooled	thoughtful
greedy	

2 For each of the words you have chosen, write
   a sentence or two explaining why you think
   that word is true for that character.

Race for the Stone!

Deep in a South American jungle lies the Temple of Ariaca. Somewhere in the temple is hidden the Stone of Fate, a fabulous jewel stolen from an Aztec city many centuries ago. Legend has it that an age of peace will follow the return of the Stone to its rightful place. The finder of the Stone shall have great riches and joy for the rest of their life.

But a dangerous and difficult journey faces those who seek the Stone, from the City of Gold high in the Peligro Mountains, by primitive railway and dirt road, then along the River Muerte through dense tropical jungle to the Temple of Ariaca itself.

The contestants

You are not alone in wanting to find the Stone. Many have tried, but perished on the way. Only the most daring and expert are now allowed to attempt the journey. Everyone who wishes to find the Stone must show documents to prove they can attempt the task.

PASSPORT

Name _Jane Jones_
Age _22_
Sex _Female_
Nationality _British_
Place of Birth _Basingstoke_

Height _1.75m_   Build _Normal_
Colour of eyes _Blue_   Colour of hair _Brown_

Distinguishing marks _None_

Signature _Jane Jones_   Date _5.6.87_

10 Downing Street,
London W 1

21st June 1988

To Whom It May Concern

This is to certify that Miss Jane 'Alligator' Jones has served the British Government in a number of dangerous situations in recent years. The most notable of these was the occasion when faced alone by an escaped lion she single-handedly wrestled it to the ground and

Buckingham Palace,
12th December 1987

My dear Miss Jones,

We are writing to you to express our sincere gratitude for the way in which you recently risked your life by diving in front of the runaway horse of one of our Lifeguards to save one of our Royal corgis. It was an act of the utmost bravery and disregard for personal safety. Please accept the small gift we enclose as a mark of our esteem.

Peter William

'Alligator' pulls it off

They said it couldn't be done. They said that she would be mad to try. But once again the amazing 'Alligator' Jones proves that 'impossible' isn't in her dictionary!

The girl who earned her nickname by wrestling with an alligator who made the mistake of choosing her for his dinner, has added yet another incredible feat to her repertoire! When the multi-storey hotel in which she was staying burst into flames trapping people on the upper floors, 'Alligator' quickly summed up the situation. She secured a rope from the roof of the hotel to the nearest building, and then in a death-defying high wire act never seen before, carried people on her shoulders across the void. 'She just whistled Waltzing Matilda and off we went,' said a grateful survivor.

Produce your passport and at least two documents to prove that you are worthy to search for the Stone: press-cuttings, letters from people for whom you have performed daring tasks, or other documents. Make sure that they are not just impressive, but genuine – the punishment for forgery is severe!

The race for the Stone

You are enjoying a train ride down the mountains. Then the train slows to a halt. A viaduct across a ravine is broken. Only the engine and one carriage can cross. How can you get all six carriages across? There is a long heavy chain in the box-car.

The train is winding its way past spectacular scenery. Suddenly it gathers speed out of control. What has happened to the driver? How can you reach the cab to put on the brakes?

Reaching the mining village at the end of the line, you decide to stay the night. Some tough characters invite you to join a poker game. You realise they will cheat. How do you get out of the game?

You can hire a car. Although the owner does look very untrustworthy, you decide to take a chance. Not far down the road, a bridge across a gorge is broken. How do you cross?

Night is falling. The fires burn brightly; your meal is cooking. Then three mean-looking hombres appear. What do they want?

You must get down the mountain. You hire a mule from a miner. It seems a good idea until you realise how stubborn a mule can be. How do you get it to move when it doesn't want to?

Safely at the top of the mountain, you admire the view. The road winds steeply down to the river station. Suddenly you realise your brakes are failing.

Your way through the jungle is across a thundering waterfall. Unless you cross it, you must backtrack miles upstream, losing valuable time. There are trees on both banks … if only you can get a rope across.

Wearily you reach the river station, looking forward to a hot bath and a good meal. Instead two policemen arrest you for stealing a car, and throw you into jail. You have to escape, but how?

Your boat sinks. Can you make a raft from its boards? What will you tie them together with? Will a raft take you through the rapids which lie ahead?

The fastest route is along the river. It lies far below, along the bottom of the ravine. Steep cliffs rise on both sides. Climbing down would take time. Diving would be fast but is the water deep enough?

You take a boat you find on the river bank. As you row, water starts to seep in. There is nothing to bail out with. As the boat lists deeper into the water, the crocodiles slide down from the banks.

Your supplies of food have run out. You realise you must make do with snake or lizard stew. But how can you catch them? **13**

You emerge from thick undergrowth into a clearing. The way looks easy ahead. You step out and begin to sink. First to your ankles, then knees, then thighs in a deadly swamp. How can you escape? Think fast! Can you use your rope? **14**

You decide the safest place to sleep is up a tree, strapped to a branch. When you awake, you discover that a band of chimps has made off with your gear. You must get it back. **15**

Congratulations! Through the jungle you catch your first sight of the Temple of Ariaca. Find the Keeper of the Temple, tell her your adventure, and ask for the Key to the Stone. Solve the riddle of this verse, Or suffer Ariaca's curse! **18**

Hacking your way through a thicket, you become entangled in a web of giant, poisonous spiders. Your machete is useless against the fine threads. The more you struggle, the tighter they cling. The spider begins to move in. **17**

A moment's carelessness, and the earth gives way beneath you. You have fallen into an animal trap. The sides are high and steep. Then, in the darkness, you hear a low growl. **16**

The Key to the Stone

The riddle of Ariaca

Four guardians of the jewel await
All who seek the stone of fate.
Death! the reward for those who fail.
Enter at the serpent's tail!
Walls! Grow jaws! Rocks! Grow teeth!
Grind to earth all who pass beneath!
Move lips of stone! Burst cheeks with air!
Blast all who Ariaca's anger dare!
Breathe mouth of flame! Lick tongues of fire!
Devour all on your deadly pyre!
If anyone the snake's head rears,
Water them with deadly tears!
Pass any through the serpent's coils,
And try to lay claim to the spoils.
Sweat of the Sun, tears of the Moon,
Do not celebrate too soon!
See the Stone! The Stone doth see!
Ariaca's venom may still fix thee!
The Stone is lost? Ariaca dies.
Perish all beneath these skies!
Let Temple fall. Earth split and crack!
Air, Fire, Water complete the wrack!
Solve the riddle of this verse,
Or suffer Ariaca's curse!

The Keeper of the Temple will only give the Key to those who have proved themselves worthy. She is blind, so each contestant must tell her their adventures in great detail, so that she can see everything clearly in her mind's eye. You must describe what you saw, heard and felt. Tell her about the places and things you have seen. Explain how you cheated death at every stage of the journey. She must live your adventures through your words.

The Key has two parts. The first part describes the plan of the Temple, but it is written in strange tribal symbols, which you will have to decode. The second part is a riddle, which hints at the dangers which will face those who enter the Temple.

1 Decode the message.
2 Study the message and the riddle together. They both contain clues to help you find the Stone and escape alive.
3 Before you dare to enter, draw a sketch plan of the Temple from the clues in the Key.
4 Decide what the dangers may be, and work out how to escape them.
5 Decide where the Stone is hidden.
6 If you escape alive, write the final chapter in your adventure, your Race for the Stone! Good luck. You will need it.

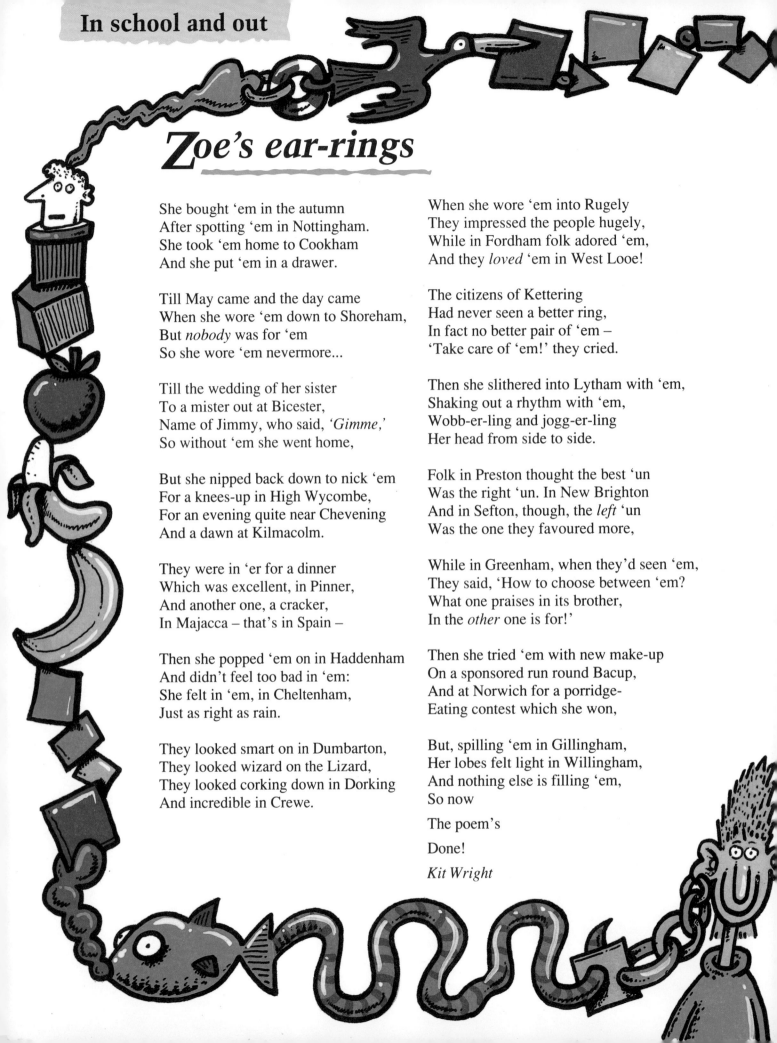

Zoe's ear-rings

She bought 'em in the autumn
After spotting 'em in Nottingham.
She took 'em home to Cookham
And she put 'em in a drawer.

Till May came and the day came
When she wore 'em down to Shoreham,
But *nobody* was for 'em
So she wore 'em nevermore...

Till the wedding of her sister
To a mister out at Bicester,
Name of Jimmy, who said, *'Gimme,'*
So without 'em she went home,

But she nipped back down to nick 'em
For a knees-up in High Wycombe,
For an evening quite near Chevening
And a dawn at Kilmacolm.

They were in 'er for a dinner
Which was excellent, in Pinner,
And another one, a cracker,
In Majacca – that's in Spain –

Then she popped 'em on in Haddenham
And didn't feel too bad in 'em:
She felt in 'em, in Cheltenham,
Just as right as rain.

They looked smart on in Dumbarton,
They looked wizard on the Lizard,
They looked corking down in Dorking
And incredible in Crewe.

When she wore 'em into Rugely
They impressed the people hugely,
While in Fordham folk adored 'em,
And they *loved* 'em in West Looe!

The citizens of Kettering
Had never seen a better ring,
In fact no better pair of 'em –
'Take care of 'em!' they cried.

Then she slithered into Lytham with 'em,
Shaking out a rhythm with 'em,
Wobb-er-ling and jogg-er-ling
Her head from side to side.

Folk in Preston thought the best 'un
Was the right 'un. In New Brighton
And in Sefton, though, the *left* 'un
Was the one they favoured more,

While in Greenham, when they'd seen 'em,
They said, 'How to choose between 'em?
What one praises in its brother,
In the *other* one is for!'

Then she tried 'em with new make-up
On a sponsored run round Bacup,
And at Norwich for a porridge-
Eating contest which she won,

But, spilling 'em in Gillingham,
Her lobes felt light in Willingham,
And nothing else is filling 'em,
So now

The poem's

Done!

Kit Wright

Hector the collector

Hector the collector
Collected bits of string,
Collected dolls with broken heads,
And rusty bells that would not ring.
Pieces out of picture puzzles,
Bent-up nails and ice-cream sticks,
Twists of wires, worn-out tyres,
Paper bags and broken bricks.
Old chipped vases, half shoe-laces,
Gatlin' guns that wouldn't shoot,
Leaky boats that wouldn't float,
And stopped-up horns that wouldn't toot.
Butter knives that had no handles,
Copper keys that fit no locks,
Rings that were too small for fingers,
Dried-up leaves and patched-up socks.
Worn-out belts that had no buckles,
'Lectric trains that had no tracks,
Airplane models, broken bottles,
Three-legged chairs and cups with cracks.
Hector the collector
Loved these things with all his soul–
Loved them more than shining diamonds,
Loved them more than glistenin' gold.
Hector called to all the people,
'Come and share my treasure trunk,'
And all the silly sightless people
Came and looked...and called it junk.

Shel Silverstein

*P*unishment

Children streamed out of the classrooms and rushed rowdily down the corridor, Miss Dabbott's voice could be heard ordering them to walk properly, and from the classroom behind the Head's study Mr Gubb appeared with a cane in his hand.

'Everyone stand still!' he bellowed. Only a few obeyed.

'Keep still all of you!' he shouted again, in a tone which none could fail to hear. This time the children nearest to him slouched to a standstill, but the others continued moving and chattering. As he strode forward to deal with them, a small boy ran out of the cloakroom, chased by a bigger one, and both blindly collided with him. He gasped with pain as the head of the smaller boy caught him in the stomach.

'You blasted idiots!' he cried; and, as they cowered back against the wall, he seized them by their shirt collars and shook them furiously. This action, and the ominous appearance of Mr Jenks, caused a cessation of movement.

Mr Jenks marched along the corridor, glaring wrathfully about him, and the children fell back on both sides without a murmur.

Mr Gubb, his round face crimson with anger, was still shaking the two major culprits.

'You two have asked for it,' he growled, 'and now you're going to get it!' He pushed them away from him. 'Hold out your hands. Both of you!' he added, when only the bigger boy obeyed. 'I hope this will be a warning to them all,' he observed to Mr Jenks, who stood grimly watching the scene at the end of the corridor.

The bigger boy was the first to be punished. He extended his left hand, but the position was not to Mr Gubb's liking.

'Get your hand higher up,' he commanded, tapping the boy's knuckles with the cane.

The boy raised his arm a few inches higher.

'Now stretch your fingers right out, unless you really want to get hurt.'

The boy stretched his fingers out to their furthest limit and held his thumb back rigidly, at right-angles to his forefinger. He stood erect with his head thrown back, his chin jutting upwards, his mouth twitching slightly in fear, but his jaw set in defiance and bravado, as John had seen men look when clumsy hands, working without anaesthetics, had probed to extract shell- splinters from their limbs. The boy's eyes were fixed on the master. He did not budge as Mr Gubb raised the cane above his shoulder and fixed his eyes on the boy's fingers with the concentration of a golfer addressing his ball. Only when the cane cracked down across his hand did the boy's nerve fail. In that moment he blinked, jerked back his head, blenched, contorted his lips, and then, as the shock was absorbed, the splinter tugged free of his flesh, his body relaxed and he casually lowered his arm. Yet his apparent unconcern was belied when he turned away from the children and cupped his hands tightly together behind him.

'Get the other hand up,' Mr Gubb directed the smaller boy, an untidy, unhealthy looking lad. 'Don't you know which is the right one yet?'

The boy lowered his arm, but instead of raising the other he looked abjectly away from Mr Gubb, and began to cry.

'What's the matter with you?' demanded Mr Gubb. 'Can't you take your medicine? Hold up your hand or worse will be coming to you.'

The boy sniffled and stammered to say something, but the words would not come.

Mr Gubb tapped his knuckles with the cane. 'Get a move on,' he said menacingly. 'Stop behaving like a girl. I haven't got time to waste on you.'

Still the boy made no effort to obey, but only sobbed the louder. His shoulders heaved and his chest shook with sobs. His nose began to water, and the grime from his lips was carried slowly downwards by the fluid in two, dirty streams which he made no effort to check.

Complete silence had fallen on the children. None of them moved. They stood tensely watching, their attention fixed on the boy. Mr Gubb made an angry move forward and seized his arm.

'If you won't do it yourself, I'll have to do it for you.'

As he straightened the boy's fingers there was a stir amongst the children, and a voice, which John knew at once to be Harkness's, called out, urgently and angrily: 'Leave my brother alone! He's got a bad hand, Sir!'

Mr Gubb dropped the boy's hand and looked up at Harkness.

'Who asked you to interfere?' he snapped.

'Nobody,' Harkness answered, coming forward, 'but he's been to hospital with that hand, and if you cane him on it, he'll have to go again.

'What's supposed to be wrong with it?'

'He had a splinter in it. It went septic, and it's not better yet.'

'If that's the case,' said Mr Gubb, turning to the victim, 'why didn't you tell me before?'

The tension in the corridor eased. John hoped that Mr Gubb would now spare the boy: but there was to be no remission; the penalty had to be paid, the example given.

'Put the other hand up,' ordered Mr Gubb.

Still sobbing, but not so wretchedly as before, the boy raised his right arm.

52

'This is one I hope you'll remember,' said Mr Gubb. He measured his distance, took up his stance, waved the cane twice above his shoulder and brought it briskly down. But before he had completed his swing the boy fearfully withdrew his arm and the cane rapped harmlessly on the floor.

'This is the last time,' Mr Gubb warned. 'If you do that again, I'll...'

'I think you'd better leave him for now,' interrupted Mr Jenks, walking down the corridor, 'I'll deal with him later.'

'I'll give him one more chance,' said Mr Gubb. He prodded the boy in the chest with the cane. 'Are you going to take it from me, or would you sooner have it from Mr Jenks?'

Without replying, the boy sniffed miserably and raised his arm. This time there was no mistake. Despite his sobs, the boy's hand remained steady. As he received the blow his face writhed and he gasped with pain. His body doubled forward and he stumbled against the wall, wringing his hands together between his knees.

Mr Gubb addressed the children, holding the cane erect against his shoulder, like a rifle. 'Let that be a lesson to you all. Don't let me catch anybody else rushing about the corridor, or they'll know what to expect. Now let me see you all get outside quietly - without any talking at all.'

Michael Croft

*C*limbing trees, dressing dolls

Why are you always tagging on?
You ought to be dressing dolls
Like other sisters.

Dolls! You know I don't like them.
Cold, stiff things lying so still.
Let's go to the woods and climb trees.
The crooked elm is the best.
From the top you can see the river
And the old man hills,
Hump-backed and hungry
As ragged beggars.
In the day they seem small and far away
But at night they crowd closer
And stand like frowning giants.
Come on! What are you waiting for?

I have better things to do.

It's wild in the woods today.
Rooks claw the air with their cackling.

The trees creak and sigh.
They say that long ago, slow Sam the woodcutter
Who liked to sleep in the hollow oak,
Was found dead there.
The sighing is his ghost, crying to come back.
Let's go and hear it.

I hate the sound.

You mean you're afraid?

Of course not.
Jim and I are going fishing.

Can I come too?

What do you know about fishing?
You're only a girl.

Olive Dove

54

Lesson poems
Drama lesson

'Let's see some super shapes you Blue Group,'
Mr Lavender shouts down the hall.
'And forests don't forget your trembly leaves
And stand up straight and tall.'

But Phillip Chubb is in our group
And he wants to be Robin Hood
And Ann Boot is sulking because she's not with
   her friend
And I don't see why I should be wood.

The lights are switched on in the classrooms,
Outside the sky's nearly black,
And the dining-hall smells of gravy and fat
And Chubb has boils down his back.

Sir tells him straight that he's got to be a tree
But he won't wave his arms around.
'How can I wave my branches, Sir,
Friar Tuck has chopped them all down.'

Then I come cantering through Sherwood
To set Maid Marion free
And I really believe I'm Robin Hood
And the Sheriff's my enemy.

At my back my trusty longbow
My broadsword clanks at my side,
My outlaws gallop behind me
As into adventure we ride.

'Untie that maid you villain,' I shout
With all the strength I have,
But the tree has got bored and is picking his nose
And Maid Marion has gone to the lav.

After rehearsals, Sir calls us together
And each group performs their play,
But just as it comes to our turn
The bell goes for the end of the day.

As I trudge my way home through the city streets
The cats and the houses retreat
And a thunder of hooves beats in my mind
And I gallop through acres of wheat.

The castle gleams white in the distance,
The banners flap, golden and red,
And distant trumpets weave silver dreams
In the landscape of my head.

Gareth Owen

Gust becos I cud not spel

Gust becos I cud not spel
It did not mean I was daft
When the boys in school red my riting
Some of them laffed
But now I am the dictater
They have to rite like me
Utherwise they cannot pas
Ther GCSE
Some of the girls wer ok
But those who laffed a lot
Have al bean rownded up
And have recintly bean shot
The teecher who corrected my speling
As not been shot at al
But four the last fifteen howers
As bean standing up against a wal
He has to stand ther until he can spel
Figgymisgrugifooniyn the rite way
I think he will stand ther forever
I just inventid it today

Brian Patten

Maths

What do you minus,
and from where?
I ask my teacher,
but he don't care.

Ten cubic metres
in square roots,
Or how many toes
go in nine boots?

Change ten decimals
to a fraction
Aaaaaaaaaaahhhhhhhhhh!
is my reaction.

Deepak Kalha

56

Lesson poems
Arithmetic

I'm 11. And I don't really know
my Two Times Table. Teacher says it's disgraceful
But even if I had the time, I feel too tired.
Ron's 5, Samantha's 3, Carole's 18 months,
and then there's Baby. I do what's required.

Mum's working. Dad's away. And so
I dress them, give them breakfast. Mrs Russell
moves in, and I take Ron to school.
Miss Eames calls me an old-fashioned word:
Dunce.
Doreen Maloney says I'm a fool.

After tea, to the Rec. Pram-pushing's slow
but on fine days it's a good place, full
of larky boys. When 6 shows on the clock
I put the kids to bed. I'm free for once.
At about 7 – Mum's key in the lock.

Gavin Ewart

How green you are!

There was a kid in our street called Julie. None of the others could stand her. She went to a different school from us, a convent school, where they had to wear uniform. The first day she went to that school, I remember, we all followed her up the road to the bus-stop, laughing at her. She looked daft. She was wearing a green school coat that was too big for her, so that her little pink hands stuck out all chubby from the sleeves, and she was weighed down with all sorts of rubbish – a shiny brown leather satchel, and a shoe-bag with a bunch of roses embroidered on it, and a hockey-stick. And she had her hair done in pigtails with green ribbons, and a stupid green hat stuck on her head.

  She went bright red when she came out of her house and saw us all waiting on the other side of the road for her. She looked as if she wanted to go back in but her mum kissed her goodbye and shut the door flat in her face and went off back to bed. So Julie smiled at us, in a half-proud, half-scared sort of way, that made her look more as if she was going to burst into tears, and marched up the street, pigtails bobbing, and over the main road to the bus-stop, and stood there gazing across at us with blank eyes while the traffic trundled backwards and forwards between us.

I wanted to shout 'Good luck Julie!' to her, but I daren't, in case the others laughed at me too. So I just stood there while they shouted 'Jolly hockey sticks,' across at her, and then Kevin started them off singing,'How green you are, how green you are, how green you are, how green...,' ever so softly, to the tune of 'Auld Lang Syne' till her bus came, and then they sang it at the tops of their voices as she staggered onto the bus and moved down to the back seat. She just sat there, staring out at us with her face all blank and closed up, as if she couldn't see us any more, and as the bus lurched forward we all waved and ran off to our big school up the hill.

But I felt a bit sad about all that. Julie had been my friend, sort of my best friend, up till then. We used to play marbles in the alley-way together, and sail paper boats down the gutter when it rained, and we'd spent all our hot summers together playing rounders on the field over the railway line and helping with the donkey-rides on the beach. It felt as if none of that had ever happened. I trailed up the hill after the others, thinking how different she looked wearing that stiff new uniform instead of her tatty little cotton dress and gym shoes. Marie was waiting for me and when I caught up with her she linked her arm in mine.

'That's her gone, the snob!' she said. 'Will you be my best friend now, Bee?'

She'd been wanting to be my best friend for ages.

And I had to say yes, because I didn't want to be called a snob too.

But I kept thinking about her during the day. It was a new school for us too, but at least we were all there together, and had been in Junior School together. It must have been really strange for her, going to a new school all on her own, and a convent school at that, with nuns like great black crows floating down the corridors and carrying her off to chapel. I was dying to know what it was like. So on my way home from school I bought a bar of Cadbury's, and I dashed to her house after tea, when none of the other kids were around. I thought we'd sit on her step, like we always did, and share out the Cadbury's, and I'd tell her about our school and she'd tell me all about the nuns and everything, but when she opened the door she just stood there, all clean and different in her stiff long uniform still, and said, 'I can't possibly play out tonight. I've got Latin homework to do.'

That did it. I ran off round to Marie's and we shared out the Cadbury's bar and then we went and played ball against Julie's house.

Marie wasn't as good as Julie, though. She was a rotten catch.

At the weekend there was a bunch of us playing down in the alley-way near Julie's house. There'd been a cowboy film on telly that afternoon and all the little ones had come out in their cowboy hats and were firing caps off at cats and down letter-boxes. Kevin and Marie and I were trying to organise them into tribes and wagon trains so we could do the film when Julie sauntered up.

'Can I play?' she said at last, after we'd ignored her about ten minutes.

I remembered the bit about the Latin homework and gave Marie half

of my last stick of bubble-gum. All the kids were watching us.

Then Kevin said, 'I bet you'd like to be an Indian Princess, wouldn't you, Julie?' Her eyes lit up. The star part! We looked at him in disgust and just stood there popping our bubble-gum while he explained to her that she had betrayed her tribe and would have to be tied to the totem-pole.

I suddenly cottoned on to what he was up to, and I ran and fetched our short washing-line, the one my mum used for dusters and tea-cloths. We tied Julie to the lamp-post with it, wound it round and round, and then the little ones all skipped round her while she did a fantastic Indian chant and vowed eternal loyalty to the tribe of Big Chief Sitting Bull. Then she started going on about her new red tap-shoes, and how the music nun wanted to teach her violin because she had such good pitch, and we all joined up in a long line, each with a hand stretched out on to the shoulder of the one in front, and we began to march round her, chanting very softly, 'How green you are, how green you are, how green you are, how green...' and then louder and louder as we danced away from her still in our long Indian file, till we got right to the top of our street where we played another game altogether, totally ignoring the yells of fury from the lamp-post, and when our mums called us in to tea we all ran in and forgot about her.

Julie couldn't forgive me for that. I used to watch her on Saturday mornings, off to dancing class, swinging her new red tap-shoes. She used to toss her head as she passed me, as if I was something nasty on the roadside that shouldn't be looked at. And then, because I stopped looking out for her, I stopped seeing her altogether. It's funny how you can spend every minute of every day with someone, and then never see her for weeks on end, just because you'd stopped even thinking about her.

I saw her one evening, quite a bit later. I'd been down the prom on my bike, and was riding up the posh part to our street. We always called it the posh part, because although our street carried on from it over the main road, it was like being in a different village altogether. They were beautiful big houses, with their own drives, and trees in the front garden. Our street was just a row of brick terrace houses, and we didn't have gardens at the front. We didn't have them at the back either, for that matter. Just little yards with w.c.'s at the bottom.

I was nearly at the top of the posh part when I saw Julie getting out of a car. She must have been given a lift home from school with someone's dad, because there were two other girls in the car in green uniforms. She said, in a funny, plummy, prim voice, 'Thank you ever so much for the lift. It was very kind of you,' and shut the car door. Then, instead of running over the main road to our street, she stood waving for a bit and then walked backwards down the posh part and started going up someone's drive. She waited there a bit and then dashed up the road and crossed over to our street. I couldn't believe it. She'd been letting on that she lived in one of those posh houses.

Soon after that I saw her big sister Barbie in Mrs Marriot's. Mrs Marriot was a woman up our street who used to sell things in her front room. It wasn't like a shop, because everything she sold she'd made herself. She'd have things in trays on their table – cakes and bread and

ginger biscuits and cough candy – but it was really queer because when you went in you couldn't smell any of the lovely things laid out on the table. All you could smell was boiled fish. They'd three cats. You sometimes got bits of cat fur stuck to your toffee-apple. Mrs Marriot was an old woman with frizzy red hair and no teeth. She was always laughing, and her gums were all pink and wet and shiny. Her husband only had one leg, and he used to sit in the corner all the time and wave his stick at you if he thought you were pinching anything.

I was standing in front of the tray of toffee-apples trying to make out which one was the biggest when Barbie came in with a jug to be filled with ginger-beer.

It was lovely, Mrs Marriot's ginger-beer. All pale and golden and powdery at the bottom.

'Why don't you go round with our Julie any more?' Barbie asked me. I went scarlet. I could feel it. She made me feel really guilty, asking me that. As if it was all my fault. Julie and I had never fallen out before, and Barbie had always been like a big sister to me, too. I liked her. I remember when she took us to the pantomime in town, and we saved up all our sweets for three weeks to give her as a present. We saved them in a big tin, and when we got to the theatre and she opened it up they were all stuck together in a fluffy lump – pear-drops and fruit-gums and licorice torpedoes and polo mints, with bits of hair and silver paper and bus tickets sticking out. Barbie said she'd rather have a cigarette anyway and gave them back to us, but we couldn't break any of them off, so we kept passing this lump backwards and forwards, sucking it and grinding little chunks off it, till we got fed up with it and chucked it on the floor. When we were going out of the theatre at the end of the pantomime I saw a little lad crawl under the seat and put it in his pocket.

I didn't know what to say to Barbie about Julie. I decided I didn't want a toffee-apple any more, even though I'd seen one with a great wedge of toffee stuck to the bottom, so I pretended I'd seen Marie passing in front of the window and I ran out and shouted, 'Wait on, Marie, I've an important message for you.' And I ran off home hoping that Barbie wouldn't come out and see that Marie wasn't there at all.

It was Kevin who told me about Julie's accident. His brother Mike used to take Barbie out on his motor-bike. They'd been engaged twice but she kept breaking it off because he couldn't hold a job down. He was working in the parks just now so he was back in, and apparently he'd had to go round and baby-sit for them the night before.

'Did you hear what happened to Julie Mills yesterday, Bee?' said Kevin, on the way to assembly.

I pretended that I did know, of course, so he didn't say anything else. 'Go on then,' I said, 'tell us.'

'She had to be rushed to hospital. She was knocked down.'

I felt as if a cold grey hand had wiped itself across my face. Kids were pushing past me down the corridor, all shouting and yelling to each other, and Kevin was carried along with them. It was like watching the tide going out. I ran after him and grabbed his arm to stop him. My legs were shaking. I could see that he was nearly bursting with excitement at having something to tell me that I didn't already know.

'What happened, Kevin? You're kidding, aren't you? You're having me on!'

'Honest! Cross me heart and hope to die. She got knocked down near her school. She went missing from class and one of the teachers went after her. When Julie saw her coming she ran off over the road. Straight into a car.'

I felt sick and faint. I didn't dare ask anything else about it. I just kept seeing her, in her pigtails and her funny long uniform coat, flying across the road and slamming into a car. And lying on the ground.

'Come on, you're not supposed to be here, young lady.' It was Mr Murphy, sweeping up all the kids hiding round the cloakrooms. 'Into assembly, this minute!' My feet just about worked, like heavy blobs at the end of bendy pipe-cleaners. I sat through assembly with all the voices and music floating over me, and every time I closed my eyes I saw Julie lying in the road.

I couldn't catch Kevin again. I could see his bright ginger head bobbing about four rows in front, and then his class all went off to the baths, and by the time he was back I was in triple needlework. I kept seeing her slamming into the car, and lying in the road, and then I saw all those black nuns floating round her and lifting her up so that her head lolled back, and I was there, wanting to say I was sorry, and her eyes were open and blank and staring right through me. Perhaps she was dead! And every time I came to that bit I jerked up in my chair and Miss Ross shouted at me. I didn't even know. I had to find out what had happened.

As soon as the bell went at the end of last lesson that morning I raced out of school. Marie yelled after me to wait but I didn't want to talk to her about it so I chucked my sandwich-box over to her and told her she could eat them for me. She couldn't believe her luck.

I ran off down the hill to our street and went down the back alley-way to Julie's, so my mum wouldn't see me. I could hardly breathe by the time I got there; my chest felt as if it was bursting and my throat was clenched tight and my legs were quivering again. I leaned against her wall and gasped for air, and my arms and legs felt like lead weights, like when you climb up out of the baths and all the water's draining off you.

I reached round and tapped on the door. I didn't know what I was going to say to Julie's mum. And I stood there, leaning against the wall with my eyes closed while I heard her trudging down the stairs and fiddling with the doorknob. And I felt her standing there.

I opened my eyes and turned round to face her. It was Julie! She was standing there in her nightie with a huge plaster across her cheek and her eye swollen and closed up, and her arm in a sling.

I stood on her doorstep and started hooting with laughter. I think she thought I was crying at first, I think I might have been, but then she started laughing too, with her face all twisted to one side as if she'd

been to the dentist, and she kept gasping and saying, 'Ooh, it hurts!
Don't make me laugh, it hurts!' Her mum came down the street
steaming from the chip shop, and she rushed us inside and got me to
make a pot of tea while she shared them all out between the three of us,
and we all sat round their fire eating them. That's the best fish and chips
I've ever had.

I felt a bit shy, going back to school, and I hovered on their doorstep
thinking what to say.

'I like your school uniform, Julie,' I said. 'I think that green suits
you.'

And she grinned at me, with her face all lop-sided. I think she
believed me.

Berlie Doherty

Zoe's ear-rings

This poem is fun to read aloud, but it is not easy to read well. You will need to practise it carefully. You could divide it up among a number of readers. If you study the lines carefully, you should be able to find interesting and entertaining ways of dividing them up.

Hector the collector

Write a collection poem of your own. It doesn't have to rhyme, but it should contain an interesting list of things - as Shel Silverstein's poem does. You can choose any topic you like, but here are two beginnings to get you going:

The caretaker

Mr Jenkins kept the school
Clean and neat and tidy
But deep inside the boiler room
He kept........

Treasure chest

My best friend's a collector
And in her room you'll find
A box that.......

Punishment

Thinking about the story

1 What arguments could you put forward for and against the use of the cane based on what you have read in this story?
2 Who do you think is the most senior of the three teachers here?

Writing

Imagine that you are Harkness and want to tell the story of the day your brother got the cane. What would you say? You might want to describe some of these things:

how your brother got into trouble
whether you thought it was fair
what you think of the school, generally
what you think of the teachers
how your brother refused to raise his arm
how you intervened
how you felt about speaking up
how the incident ended
what happened on the way home that night.

Climbing trees, dressing dolls

Thinking about the poem

1 What is going on at the beginning of the poem?
2 What do you think has happened before the poem begins?
3 Do you think the boys are afraid? (What are your reasons?)
4 What do you think will happen next?

Writing a story

You are one of the people in the poem. Tell your story, based on the poem.
Before you write, think about these things:

● What kind of person am I?
● What do I think and feel about the others?
● How did all this happen?
● What happens next?
● What happens?

Lesson poems

Thinking about the poems

1 Which did you like best and why?
2 Did any of them describe experiences like those you have had?
3 If you were going to write about something at school, what would you choose and why?
4 Choose one of the poems to read aloud. Practise reading it and think up a few sentences to explain why you have chosen it.

Your writing

Write about your thoughts and feelings about a school subject. Either use your own approach, or choose from this list:

1 A poem that ends with the words, Aaaaaaaaaahhhhhhhhhh! is my reaction.
2 A poem about a lesson that uses speech and storytelling, as *Drama Lesson* does.
3 A poem about *The Pupil's Revenge*.

How green you are!

Thinking about the story

1 Why did all the children laugh at Julie on the first day she went to her new school?
2 How do you think Julie felt that day?
3 Did you feel sorry for her then?
4 Did you feel sorry for her later in the story?
5 When Julie was left tied to the lamp post was it fair, unfair, cruel...or what?
6 Whose fault was it that Julie and Bee stopped seeing each other?
7 Why did Julie get hurt and what effect did it have on Bee?
8 What were your feelings at the end?

Writing

We see this story through Bee's eyes. We have to work out some of the things that happened to Julie – and what her thoughts and feelings were. What was her version of the story?

1 Make a list of the main things that happened to her in the story. Number them.
2 For each one write down what she thought and felt. (You can use the numbers to help you keep track of things.)
3 Use these lists and tell 'Julie's story'. Write as if you were Julie.

Monsters of the deep

The next four pages contain the parts of the book that the boy was reading. Read them for yourself and decide who is right.

1 Explain who you think is right and why. (Pick out the parts of the book which make you think this.)

2 The boy and the girl continue their argument, pointing out the parts of the book that back up what they are saying. Which parts does each one point out?

3 Write the rest of the argument.

How would you explain?

Use the information on the next four pages to write a short description of each of these three things suitable for a five-year-old brother or sister.

Telling the story

The four pages contain a number of stories describing people's encounters with sea monsters of different kinds.

Either Choose one of these and tell the whole story of what happened – as if you were one of the people in the story. (Write as 'I'.)

Or Make up a story about meeting a sea monster. Write as if it happened to you.

Read all about it !

1 The Captain of the Rebecca Sims kept a ship's log. In it he described all the things that happened on the voyage. Write the Captain's log for the period that starts when they first saw the strange 'whale' and ends when he saw the Monongahela for the last time.

2 When the only survivor from the American Air Force raft got back to Florida, he was interviewed by excited press reporters. Write the newspaper report of the disaster.

Serpents in the sea

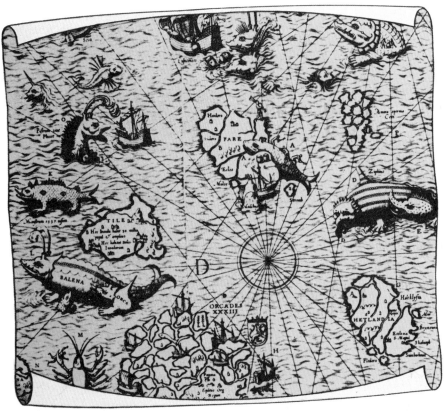

Oceans cover more than two-thirds of the earth's surface, and in places reach a depth of eleven kilometres. This underwater world has not yet been thoroughly explored, so it is possible that unknown monsters exist there.

Between the 17th century and the present day, there have been hundreds of detailed sightings of terrifying creatures at sea. These are most often described as giant squid and octopuses (see pages 18-19) or as "sea serpents".

Reports of sea serpents say they look like smooth snakes, but they are many times larger than the biggest snakes on earth: the longest seem to be about 200 metres.

They are said to be yellow or mottled brown in colour, often with seaweed-like manes. Their heads can be up to three metres long, equipped with curving teeth. They seem to have neither fins nor limbs, and they twist and turn through the water like snakes.

▲ In the 16th century, when this map was made, little was known about creatures that lived in remote areas of the globe. Map-makers decorated their maps with imaginary beasts.

▶ The serpent found by *Monongahela's* crew may have looked like this. Mariners' tales, often exaggerated by retelling, are the main source of information about sea monsters.

Monongahela's monster

In 1852, two whaling ships, the *Monongahela* and the *Rebecca Sims*, from New Bedford (see map on right), were sailing alongside each other in the Pacific. A look-out reported a whale off the port bow. The master of the *Monongahela*, Captain Seabury, launched three longboats to go after it.

As they drew near their prey, the sailors realized that they were dealing with something much more fierce than any whale. Seabury nevertheless decided to tackle it, and thrust a harpoon deep into the creature's neck. It died within minutes, but not before sinking the other two longboats with its threshings

The sailors hauled in their amazing catch. The captain of the *Rebecca Sims* described it in the ship's log as a brownish-grey reptile at least 45 metre long. In its great jaws were dozens of sharp and curving teeth.

The body was too large to bring on board, so the head was cut off and preserved in a pickling vat aboard the *Monongahela*.

The monster is lost

The two ships then started back for their home port. The *Rebecca Sims* returned safely, but the other ship was never seen again. No trace of its crew, nor of the monster's head, was ever found. Only some wreckage was wash up, off the coast of Alaska.

Monongahela's route

NORTH
AMERICA

New
Bedford

Serpent
sighted
here

Whaling
grounds

SOUTH
AMERICA

Route of the
Monongahela

The North Sea Terror

In 1881, a Scottish fishing boat, the *Bertie,*
was 140 kilometres out in the North Sea.
Suddenly, the crew noticed three humps
breaking the surface of the water, and
then part of a head draped with a growth
that looked like seaweed. Two fierce eyes
glared at the terror-stricken sailors.

The creature headed straight for the
boat. The crew tried to drive it away, and
one man fired a rifle at it. The "serpent"
churned the water, almost capsizing the
boat.

Fishing gear was thrown off the deck
and two of the crew were pitched
violently backwards into the hold.

The fishermen cut their lines and set
sail for port, but the sea serpent
continued to follow them. When night
fell, the crew lost sight of the strange
monster.

Panic in the fog

In 1962, off the Florida coast, an
American Air Force raft, carrying five
skin-divers, was swept out to sea in a
storm. As the storm cleared, dense fog
came down.

After they had been stranded for
about an hour, they heard splashing and
noticed a smell of dead fish, then a
hissing noise. Suddenly, what looked like
a brown, slimy neck, about four metres
long, reared up out of the water. The
creature's head was shaped like a sea
turtle's. One diver saw the neck bend and
the head dip into the water several times.
The divers panicked and leapt into the
sea. In the fog, they lost sight of one
another. According to the only survivor,
his comrades went under one by one,
screaming in terror. They were
never found.

The riddle of the Kraken

"Kraken" is an old Norse word used to describe giant sea creatures that mariners reported they had seen. They were said to be shaped like squid or octopuses, with many arms that could pluck men from ships, and even drag whole boats to the bottom of the sea.

Although many of the stories are exaggerated accounts, and were once thought to be only legends, there is now proof that giant squid do exist. Parts of squid and even whole bodies of enormous size have been found. They have been examined by experts in many different parts of the world.

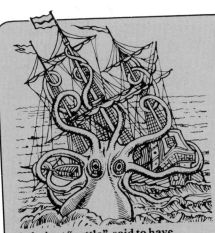

▲ A giant "cuttle", said to have wrapped its tentacles round the masts of an 18th-century slave ship.

Fight with a kraken

In 1873, two men and a boy were fishing in a rowing boat off the coast of Newfoundland, when one of the men stuck a boathook into a mass of floating wreckage. Suddenly, the "wreckage" jerked to life. It was an enormous sea monster. Two of its tentacles shot out to grasp the little boat.

The creature began to sink beneath the water, pulling the boat along with it. As the sea flooded around them, the boy grabbed an axe and hacked at the slithery tentacles. As he cut at them, the monster released a jet of black ink, withdrew and disappeared.

The fishermen reached the shore unharmed and took a piece of tentacle to show to a local naturalist called Moses

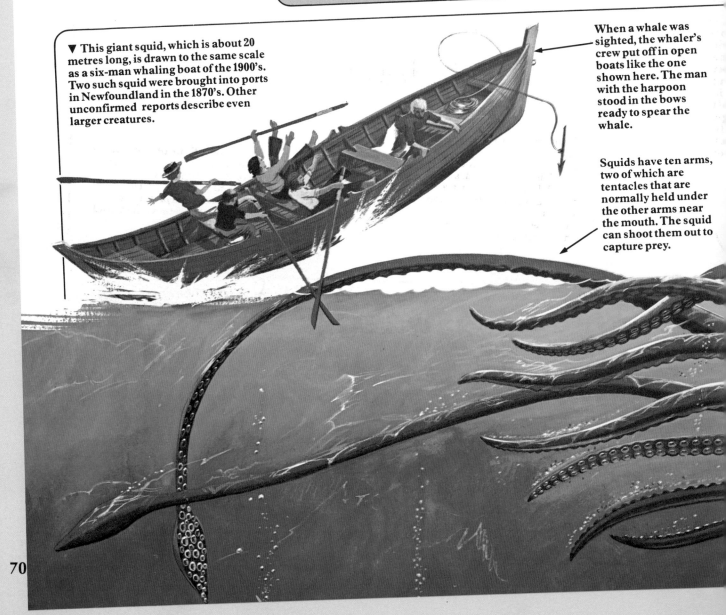

▼ This giant squid, which is about 20 metres long, is drawn to the same scale as a six-man whaling boat of the 1900's. Two such squid were brought into ports in Newfoundland in the 1870's. Other unconfirmed reports describe even larger creatures.

When a whale was sighted, the whaler's crew put off in open boats like the one shown here. The man with the harpoon stood in the bows ready to spear the whale.

Squids have ten arms, two of which are tentacles that are normally held under the other arms near the mouth. The squid can shoot them out to capture prey.

rvey. He was amazed by the
cimen, which was very tough and six
tres long.

re proof is found

nonth later, four other men brought
rvey a similar creature. They said
y had been bringing in one of their
s, which had seemed very heavy.
en they got it to the surface, they had
n a writhing mass of jelly, from which
o fierce eyes had peered at them. They
d battled with it until one of them
led it.
Moses Harvey bought the creature
m the fishermen for ten dollars. He
ok several photographs of it and sent
em off to London. There, scientists
o examined it declared that it was a
giant squid—one of the largest ever
found.

In 1887, another giant squid was
found, this time in New Zealand. Its body
measured about 3 metres, and its
tentacles were another 13 metres long.
As recently as 1964, an 11-metre squid
was found in the sea near La Coruna,
in Spain.

Monsters of the deep

Even today, we do not know exactly how
large squid can grow. One estimate is
based on the size of marks found on the
heads of some sperm whales (who
eat mainly squid). These are scars left
by the squids' suckers on the whales'
skin. The whales seem to have fought
with squid at least 25 metres long.

▲ A sea monster described in a book
in the 16th century.

squid is an
vertebrate (an animal
ithout a backbone),
hat is related to the
ctopus and the
uttlefish. Squid have
ircular suckers on each
f their arms. As well as
iant squid like this one,
here are small ones,
bout 20 centimetres
ong.

Giant squid live in deep open
water, but may come to the
surface of the sea in search of
food. Their diet includes
shellfish and fish. They are
pursued and eaten by toothed
whales. Bodies of giant squid
have been found in sperm
whales' stomachs.

The squid can contract
its body suddenly,
forcing out a strong
jet of water, which
propels it backwards.
It can also squirt
out ink to confuse its
enemies.

▲ Some people think that the idea of
sea serpents arose from sightings of
giant squid. If a squid was under the
water, and raised one tentacle above
the surface, as in this picture, this
could appear to be a snake-like head
and neck.

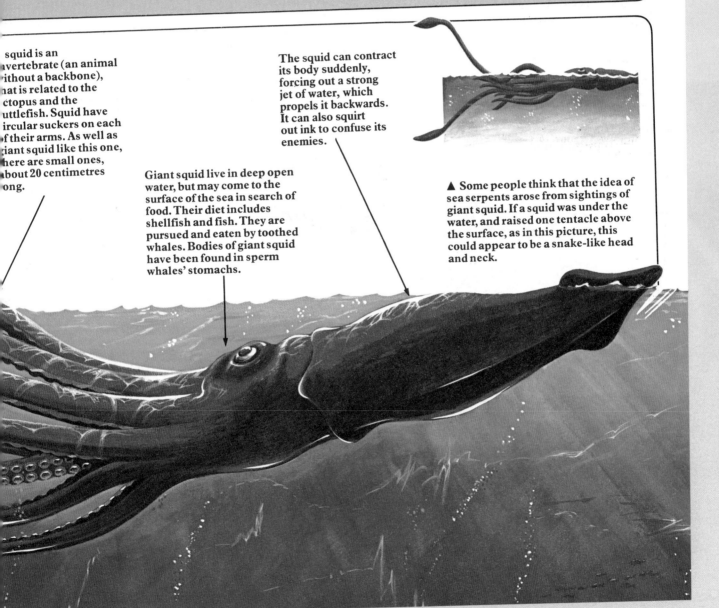

The farmer's wife and the tiger

A tale from Pakistan

One day a farmer went with his oxen to plough his field. He had just turned the first furrow when a tiger walked up and said: 'Peace be with you, friend. How are you this fine morning?'

'The same to you, my lord, and I am pretty well, thank you,' replied the farmer, quaking with fear but thinking it wisest to be polite.

'I am glad to hear it, because Heaven has sent me to eat your two oxen,' said the tiger cheerfully. 'You are a God-fearing man, I know, so make haste and unyoke them.'

'Aren't you making a mistake, my lord?' asked the farmer. His courage had returned now that he knew the tiger was only proposing to gobble up his oxen, not him. 'Heaven sent me to plough this field, and in order to do so, I must have oxen. Hadn't you better go and make further enquiries?'

'There is no need to delay, and I should be sorry to keep you waiting,' said the tiger. 'If you'll unyoke the oxen, I'll be ready in a moment to eat them.' With that the tiger began to sharpen his teeth and claws in a very frightening manner.

The farmer begged and prayed that his oxen might not be eaten and promised that, if the tiger would spare them, he would give in exchange a fine fat young milk cow of his wife's.

To this the tiger agreed, and taking the oxen with him for safety, the farmer hurried home. Seeing him return so early from the fields, his wife, who was an energetic, hard-working woman, called out: 'What! Lazy bones! Back already and my work just beginning!'

The farmer explained how he had met the tiger and how, to save his oxen, he had promised the cow in exchange. At this his wife began to shout, saying: 'A likely story indeed! What do you mean by saving your stupid oxen at the expense of my beautiful cow! Where will the children get milk? How can I cook without butter?'

'All very fine, wife,' retorted the farmer, 'but how can we make bread without grain? How can we have grain without oxen to plough the fields? It's surely better to do without milk and butter than without bread. So make haste and untie the cow.'

'You great silly!' scolded his wife. 'If you had an ounce of sense in your brain, you'd think of some plan to get us out of our difficulty!'

'Think of one yourself!' cried her husband in a rage.

'So I will!' replied his wife. 'But if I do the thinking, you must obey me, for I can't do both. Go back to the tiger and tell him that the cow wouldn't come with you, but that your wife is bringing it.'

The farmer, who was a great coward, didn't like the idea of going back empty-handed to the tiger, but as he could not think of any other plan, he did as he was told. He found the tiger still sharpening his claws and teeth, he was so hungry. When he heard that he had to wait still longer for his dinner, he began to growl and lash his tail and curl his whiskers in a most terrible manner causing the poor farmer's knees to knock together with terror. Now, when the farmer had left the house, his wife went out to the stable and saddled the pony. Then she put on her husband's best clothes, tied the turban high so as to look as tall as possible, jumped astride the pony, and set off to the field where the tiger was waiting.

She rode along, swaggering like a man, till she came to where the lane turned into the field, and there she called out as bold as brass: 'Now, please the powers I may find a tiger in the field! I haven't tasted tiger since yesterday when I ate three for breakfast.'

Hearing these words and seeing the speaker ride boldly toward him, the tiger was so alarmed that he turned tail and bolted into the forest. He went at such a headlong pace that he nearly knocked down his own jackal – tigers always have a jackal of their own to clear away the bones after they have finished eating.

'My lord! My lord!' cried the jackal. 'Where are you going so fast?'

'Run! Run!' panted the tiger. 'There's the very devil of a horseman in yonder field who thinks nothing of eating three tigers for breakfast!'

At this the jackal laughed behind his paw. 'My dear master,' he said, 'the sun has dazzled your eyes! That was no horseman, but only the farmer's wife dressed up as a man!'

'Are you quite sure?' asked the tiger, pausing in his flight.

'Quite sure, my lord,' said the jackal, 'and if your lordship's eyes had not been dazzled – ahem – by the sun, your lordship would have seen the woman's pigtail hanging down behind her.'

'But you may be mistaken,' persisted the cowardly tiger, 'she was the very devil of a horseman to look at!'

'Who's afraid!' replied the jackal. 'Come! Don't give up your dinner because of a woman! We'll go together.'

'No! You might take me there and then run away and leave me!' said the tiger fearfully.

'Well, let us tie our tails together then, so that I can't!' suggested the cunning jackal. He was determined not to be done out of his bones at the end of the feast.

To this the tiger agreed, and having tied their tails together in a reef knot, the pair set off arm in arm.

Now the farmer and his wife had remained in the field, laughing over the trick they had played on the tiger. Suddenly, lo and behold, what

should they see but the tiger and the jackal coming toward them with their tails tied together.

'Run!' cried the farmer. 'We are lost! We are lost!'

'Nothing of the kind, you great baby,' answered his wife coolly. 'Stop that noise! I can't hear myself speak!'

She waited until the pair of animals was within hail, then called out politely: 'How very kind of you, dear Mr Jackal, to bring me such a nice fat tiger! I shan't be a moment finishing off my share of him, and then you can have the bones.'

At these words the tiger became wild with fright and, quite forgetting the jackal and the reef knot in their tails, he bolted away full tilt, dragging the jackal behind him. Bumpety, bump, bump, over the stones! Scritch, scratch, scramble, through the thorny bushes!

In vain the poor jackal howled and shrieked to the tiger to stop, but the noise behind him only frightened the coward more. Away he went, helter-skelter, hurry-scurry, over hill and dale, till he was nearly dead with fatigue, and the jackal was quite dead from bumps and bruises.

And the farmer and his wife were never troubled by the tiger again.

Retold by *Ikram Chunghtai*
Translated by *Ikram Chunghtai* and *S Afaq Ahmed*

Why cassowaries don't fly

Rima stepped back and looked critically at his handiwork. He grunted with satisfaction, and smiled down at his son.

'Well?'

The new hut stood foursquare in the corner of the garden. The plaited bamboo walls curled tightly round a stout frame of beech poles, cut and stripped by Rima with the big bush knife he had brought up from the trade-store when Joseph had run down to tell him the news.

'It's marvellous, father,' said Joseph. 'She won't get out of that.'

He bent down and stroked the shining plumage of a large bird that lay at his feet, trussed up with creepers. The bonds were too tight to allow the muscular body any movement, but the bird crossly jerked its head and opened its pointed beak to hiss at Joseph's fingers. The face and neck were coloured bright blue and red, and the head was topped with an oval dome of bone. The feathers were long and limp, hanging in silky strands. Under the creeper bindings twitched stumps of flightless wings.

'That's a fine cassowary,' Rima remarked. 'Did she give you much trouble?'

'No: after all, there were eight of us. Aieee! She ran like the wind!'

The village boys had caught the cassowary that morning, coming on her suddenly in the bush and chasing her down a long slope. Her strong legs were capable of taking her clear of pursuers on the level or going

uphill. But once she was on a downward incline she could only run faster and faster, squawking with fury as she lost her balance, till she tripped over and fell in a tumble of feathers and feet.

Then Joseph and another boy, outrunning the others, had flung themselves on top of the flapping bird and held her down, while the remaining young hunters had torn down bush creepers for rope. The trickiest part was keeping the feet with their fearsome claws underneath the body while she was lashed up like a parcel. The whooping and laughing boys carried her back to the village, her head dangling down from a branch slotted between her feet. Joseph and the other boy had drawn playing cards for her, and Joseph's ten of hearts had just beaten David Mali's nine of diamonds.

Joseph was overjoyed to have his own cassowary. She would always be bad-tempered, liable to peck out an eye or lash out dangerously with those sharp claws. But safely shut in her new home, fed on taro scraps and berries, she would grow fat; and one day in the future she would make a tough but tasty roast for a clan gathering. Then the story of the capture would be told, with Joseph as the hero.

'Ready? Let's get her inside. I'll hold her, and you cut the ropes – here, take my knife. Watch out, now – she's in a bad mood.'

Rima picked up the cassowary in his strong arms and clasped the hard thigh muscles with both hands while Joseph sawed through the creepers. The big bird squatted quietly against Rima's chest, but her eyes held a sulky, defiant glare. Rima waddled with his burden towards the little hut, which he had purposely built without a door; the cassowary would not be coming out again before her day of doom. A small window about four feet from the ground provided the only

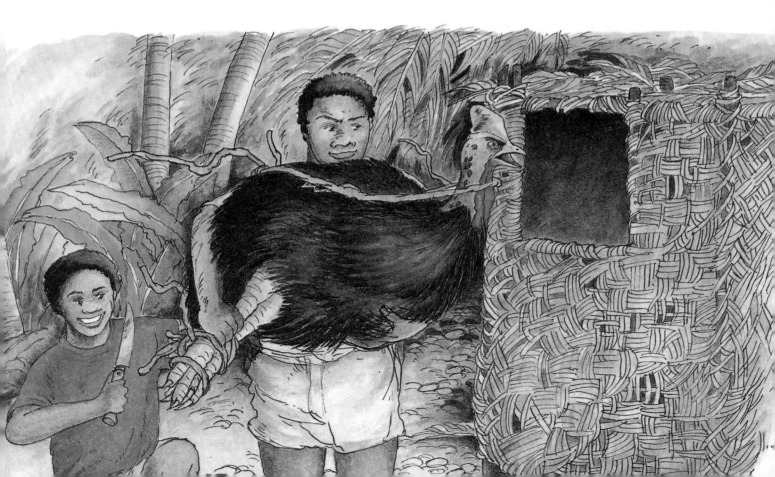

entrance, and Rima rested the bird's weight against the frame while Joseph stood on tiptoe beside him to watch.

With a heave of both arms and chest Rima pushed the cassowary through the window. As she fell into the dark interior of the hut, one cramped leg came free for a moment, and in that split second the bird kicked out viciously. The long middle claw on her foot tore a gash in Rima's arm and spots of blood began to well up on the brown skin.

'Ai!'

Rima cursed, and brushed away the blood with his other hand. He grabbed Joseph roughly by the shoulder as the boy peered in at the window, and pulled him away.

'Get back! Do you want to lose an eye?'

From the inside of the hut came a thumping and screeching as the cassowary tested her dungeon. The whole building shook, and some grass fell from the roof; but Rima had built many cassowary huts, and this one stood up sturdily to the battering.

The window was too high up to be reached by the captive, though she could poke her head out to be fed. If these huts were strongly constructed, they made a foolproof prison for a flightless bird.

Rima rubbed his wounded arm.

'Give her some food and water tonight, when she's tired herself out,' he advised. 'But be careful, Joseph! Never trust one of those brutes.'

He inspected the scratch. It was sore, but would heal up cleanly in a few days.

'Lucky it wasn't a male in the breeding season!'

'Why?' Joseph asked his favourite question.

'All that hot blood goes to their feet, that's why. Their main claws swell up like a rotten log. In the old days you were done for. Even now there are a few people waking up in Goroka hospital with only one arm, wishing they hadn't got between Mr Cassowary and his girl-friends.'

Joseph glanced up at his father as they walked down the path to the village. As usual, he wasn't sure whether Rima was joking. But his father's face was quite serious.

'You ask your grandfather about it tonight. He can tell you a tale or two about our friend in the hut.'

Rima looked at the sun as it hung above the mountain tops.

'Come on, boy. I must get this scratch washed and tied up. Jipona will be waiting for you, too. Run!'

Kian Kombruk drew on his cigarette until the end glowed red.

'How did she like her supper?' he asked his grandson. Joseph hugged his knees by the fire.

'She ate it all, grandfather – at least I think she did. I didn't dare look in to see!'

Everyone laughed. Joseph ducked his head behind his arm, embarrassed. But Kian went on kindly, 'I hear you were a little bolder in the bush this morning. It was a brave thing to do, jumping on a cassowary in full flight.'

'A foolish thing to do,' murmured Jipona. 'He might have really hurt himself.'

'I remember the first time I tried that,' said Kian. 'The old bird we were chasing just put on an extra spurt, and I banged my chin on the ground so hard I thought a tree had fallen on me!' The old man scratched his beard thoughtfully. 'It's lucky they can't fly; otherwise we'd never get near them. And a cassowary's wing-bone through the nose of a handsome young fellow was a fine attraction for the girls once upon a time!'

Kian fingered the hole that his own father had pierced through the fleshy part of his nose between the nostrils when Kian had reached manhood. Joseph had seen his grandfather dressed up for a sing-sing with a long white bone through this hole, forming a kind of false moustache each side of his nose.

'But there was a time long ago when the cassowary could fly as well as the bower-bird,' the old man rumbled as he reached for a sweetcorn in the cinders.

Cassowary and Bower-bird used to fly around together. Any morning you could see them tearing through the tree-tops, chasing each other up and down as they searched for the red berries that they loved. These berries, plump and sweet, grew on the bushes near the very top of the mountain. All the birds in the forest knew about them; but they took good care to keep away when Cassowary and Bower-bird came racketing through the jungle.

Bower-bird was normally a shy fellow, who lived deep in the bush in a little house he had made from leaves and moss, and decorated with brightly-coloured pebbles and flowers. He kept himself to himself, and never bothered anyone. Then he struck up an acquaintance with

79

Cassowary, and began to puff out his chest and give a beak-full of cheek to everyone he met; even to wise old Owl himself! Cassowary taught him bad habits, but Cassowary didn't care – not he! All he wanted was a belly-full of berries and a chance to bully the small birds. When he flapped his stumpy wings and heaved his fat body up above the topmost branches, Cassowary was as pleased as pie. He sang as he flew – a croaking song, horrible to hear – but Cassowary didn't care. Not he! He smashed up the nests of the Birds of Paradise, and flew off laughing.

'That Cassowary will come to a bad end,' grunted old Owl when he heard of the goings-on. 'He's a sight too full of himself. He'll trip over his own wings one fine day, mark my words.'

One day Cassowary flopped down into the clearing in front of Bower-bird's pretty little house.

'What's new?' he screeched.

'There's a batch of bushes in berry on the morning side of the mountain,' said Bower-bird. 'I saw them when I flew over yesterday.'

Cassowary's little eyes sparkled with greed. The two companions flew off and were soon high above the jungle, cruising towards the mountain.

'Doesn't he look a fool?' sniggered the ground pigeons as the pair went overhead. Cassowary did look decidedly odd with his short wings flailing like paddles to keep his heavy body aloft, and his long legs treading the air beneath him. All the same, the ground pigeons were careful to keep well under cover. They had tasted Cassowary's sharp dagger of a beak before.

Soon the two partners had landed on the mountain top, and they got busy among the berry bushes. Bower-bird ate daintily, plucking one scarlet berry at a time from its bed of leaves, chewing it thoroughly in his short beak and swallowing before taking another. Cassowary behaved like the ruffian that he was, tearing away whole clusters of berries and gorging them all at once, champing and crashing among the bushes. He spoiled twice as much fruit as he ate by crushing the berries beneath his clumsy feet in a mad rush from bush to bush. Bower-bird began to get impatient.

'Do be careful, Cassowary,' he twittered peevishly. 'You're wasting half of them!'

The only reply was a muffled crunching as Cassowary disposed of a beak-full of berries, leaves and twigs. He ripped the last few berries off their bush, swallowed them in one gulp, and surveyed the mess he had made with satisfaction.

'That was good! What's next?' he demanded.

Bower-bird was furious. The berries had been his discovery, after all, and he had eaten hardly a dozen.

'It's time you learned a lesson, my friend,' he muttered under his breath. Looking around, his glance fell on the twigs scattered on the ground where Cassowary had thrown them. Now Bower-bird, for all his small size, was a quick-witted fellow, and at once he thought of a trick to play on Cassowary.

'I'll show you what's next,' he thought, and turned to Cassowary with his sweetest smile. 'Er – why not sing me one of your lovely songs?'

Like many bullies, Cassowary was extremely vain. He loved the sound of his own singing, though no-one else did. He preened himself and smirked.

'Let's fly up into that tree over there,' suggested Bower-bird, 'then the whole forest could enjoy your wonderful voice.'

Cassowary lumbered up on to a branch and began to squawk, screwing his eyes tight shut, the better to appreciate his own performance. Bower-bird picked up two green twigs and hid them under his wings. Then he flew up beside Cassowary and pretended to be listening to the song. At last the big bully grated to a stand-still, and opened his eyes to see the effect on his little friend.

'Wonderful! Quite marvellous!' enthused Bower-bird. 'They must have heard you over in Wabag. Truly the cassowaries have the loudest – er, I mean the loveliest – voices in all the world!'

'Yes, my family are very gifted,' sighed Cassowary. 'We are strong, brave, clever – and the gods have blessed us with magical voices, too.'

He looked down at the little bird beside him. 'It's a pity they seem to have forgotten you, my dear fellow. All you can do is poke bits of coloured stone about, eh?'

Bower-bird saw that his chance had come.

'Well, actually – that's not quite all we can do.'

He lowered his voice and glanced over his shoulder. 'In fact, I'll let you into a secret, if you like. We're not supposed to tell anyone about it, but I don't mind you knowing.'

'Oh, I won't tell a soul,' promised the delighted Cassowary.

'Bend your head down here,' murmured Bower-bird. Cassowary put his domed head close to Bower-bird's beak.

'We can break our bones and heal ourselves straight away,' whispered the little bird. 'All the Bower-birds can do it.'

Cassowary straightened up and stared disbelievingly at him. 'Break your bones and heal yourself? Nonsense! No-one can do that. I've never heard such rubbish!'

'It's true,' Bower-bird said, nodding his head.

'Prove it, then,' jeered Cassowary. 'You're just making it up!'

Bower-bird smiled to himself. 'Very well,' he answered. 'Suppose I were to break the bones in my wings, and then fly to the top of the mountain and back. Would you believe me then?'

'If you can do that,' conceded Cassowary, 'I'll believe you – but you can't!'

Bower-bird sidled along the branch away from Cassowary. He didn't want the big fool overlooking his preparations. Pretending to mutter magic words to distract Cassowary's attention, he adjusted the green twigs under his wings. The he began to press the twigs against the branch, groaning loudly and jabbering incantations. The twigs bent under the pressure, then splintered with a tearing crack.

Cassowary blinked in astonishment. It certainly seemed as if his friend had snapped the bones of both his wings. Then he gaped as Bower-bird fluttered the wings that should have been useless, and sprang into the air in a perfect take-off. Straight and fast flew Bower-bird as he made for the mountain top. Cassowary was too far away to see the two splintered twigs that fell from beneath the trickster's wings and vanished among the tree-tops. Bower-bird rolled and swooped to show off his flying skills before returning to land beside Cassowary on the branch. For once in his life, Cassowary was speechless.

Bower-bird smiled mockingly at him. 'Now it's your turn,' he said. 'Come on – all you have to do is break your wings and fly! I'll say the magic words for you. Or are you scared?'

This suggestion went straight to the foolish Cassowary's head, as the cunning Bower-bird had planned. He looked down at his own stubby wings, while Bower-bird began to chant gibberish. Break his wing-bones? Well – if a little squirt of a bower-bird could do it – so could a cassowary!

He pressed the tips of his wings against the branch and leaned his full weight on them.

'Ow! Ow! It hurts!'

'That's only because you've had no practice,' Bower-bird said

reassuringly. He choked back his laughter as he watched the wincing Cassowary bending his wings.

'I thought you were good at everything. The ground pigeons will laugh themselves sick when I tell them you couldn't even break your own bones – you've broken enough of theirs!'

This prospect made Cassowary mad with rage. He jerked downwards with the powerful muscles of his shoulders. Snap! went the bones of his wings.

'Ai! Aieeee!' squealed Cassowary.

'Now, my good friend – fly!' shouted Bower-bird, and gave the heavy body a hard push. Cassowary rocked and swayed, digging his toes desperately into the branch. Then he lost his balance and fell backwards, tumbling like a sack of yams to the ground below.

Bower-bird opened his beak, threw back his head and laughed until the tears came.

'Oh, Cassowary – why don't you fly?' he called down. Cassowary heaved about in the grass. He got to his feet and tried to fly up to get at Bower-bird, but every time he leaped into the air he fell back to earth.

'You devil! You've tricked me! I can't fly!' wailed Cassowary. 'Just wait till I get up there!'

He took a run at the tree trunk, and scrambled a few feet up before pitching on his head. Bower-bird laughed and laughed.

'Eh, great flyer! Why don't you fly? Eaten too many berries?'

Just then a man, attracted by all the noise and commotion, came out of the jungle and began to climb up the mountainside towards Cassowary.

'Here's a friend for you, Cassowary,' chortled Bower-bird. 'Ask him if he knows the magic words! Farewell, great flyer!'

Then Bower-bird spread his wings and flew away to tell the world the news of the downfall of Cassowary. Old Owl mumbled, 'I knew it! He tripped over his own wings, just as I said.'

And the wise old bird, who had seen many a bully brought low in the twenty years since he was hatched, clicked his beak and closed his eyes.

Christopher Somerville

She called it her robin

She called it her robin.
And once she took me to see.
All she did
Was outstretch her hand
And sprinkle
Cheese crumbs
On the palm.
She would call softly,
'Robby, Robby.'
Nothing happened at first,
But then,
A rose bush
Sprang to life
As her robin,
Wings vibrating,
Flew from his nest in the roots.

He landed, delicately,
On her palm.
His breast was brick red,
The edges a musty orange.
Fading into the brown of his back.
His eyes shone,
Chips of wet flints
Smoothed round.
His beak was like the tip
Of a rose thorn
As he pecked for the cheese.

She spoke to him soothingly,
Dragging out the vowel sounds,
'Robby, my little Robby,'
The tip of her little finger
Tracing down his back
As she lovingly stroked
Her fickle friend.

Lara Mair (12)

84

Litany

I hold the splendid
daylight in my hands
Inwardly grateful for
a lovely day.
Thank you life.
Daylight like a fine
fan spread from my
hands
Daylight like scarlet
poinsettias
Daylight like yellow
cassia flowers
Daylight like clean
water
Daylight like green
cacti
Daylight like sea
sparkling with white
horses
Daylight like tropic
hills
Daylight like a
sacrament in my
hands
Amen.

George Campbell

Rainbow

When you see
de rainbow
you know
God know
wha he doing –
one big smile
across the sky –
I tell you
God got style
the man got style
When you see
raincloud pass
and de rainbow
make a show
I tell you
is God doing
limbo
the man doing
limbo

But sometimes
you know
when I see
de rainbow
so full of glow
and curving
like she bearing a child
I does want know
if God
ain't a woman
If that is so
the woman got style
man she got style

John Agard

The farmer's wife and the tiger

Thinking about the story

As you read this story your ideas about the four characters develop and change. Copy and complete this table:

Character	What I thought about this character when s/he first appeared.	What I thought about this character at the end of the story.
Farmer		
Farmer's wife		
Tiger		

Writing

The farmer's wife is obviously good at solving problems. Think about her character and about how she solved the problem.

Now think about how she might solve this problem:

The farmer's land belongs to a rich landlord. He is old and when he dies his selfish son inherits the land. He tells the farmer and his wife he wants four times as much rent for the land. If they do not pay, he will take the land back and sell it to a rich friend. What are they to do? They cannot afford the extra rent and if they are driven away they will starve.

Why cassowaries don't fly

Thinking about the story

This story is really made up of two stories:
-    A How Rima caught and caged the cassowary
-    B How the Bower-bird tricked the Cassowary.

A 1 What is the background to the story?
  - where do the people live?
  - what is their life like?
  - when did it all happen?
2 Why is Rima so pleased to have his own cassowaries?
3 What are cassowaries like?
4 What do you think of the way the people treat cassowaries?

B 1 How does the story describe the character of the Cassowary?
2 What is the Bower-bird like?
3 What makes the Bower-bird decide to trick the Cassowary?
4 Do you think the Cassowary deserves to be tricked in this way? What are your reasons?

The trial of the Bower-bird

Not all the birds agree that the cassowary deserved to be treated in this way. They decide that the Bower-bird must go on trial. You are going to tell the story of what happened. Begin by thinking of the answers to these questions:

1 What do you think Bower-bird could be accused of? (The charge)
2 Who would be the judge?
3 What would be the main points against the Bower-bird? (The prosecution case)
4 What would be the main points in his defence? (The defence case)
5 What would the result be? (The verdict)

Now tell the story. It should contain these four parts:

1 The judge states the charge.
2 The Cassowary (or another bird) states the prosecution case.
3 The Bower-bird (or another bird) states the defence case.
4 The judge delivers the verdict.

Litany

A litany is a kind of prayer which is often like a list. Each thing on the list begins in the same way. This makes a good pattern for a poem, too. You can use a similar pattern for your own poems:

Daylight
Daylight like -
Daylight like
Daylight like -
Daylight like
Daylight like -
Amen.

Instead of *Daylight*, you could use *Sunshine*, or *Water*, or *Friendship* – or choose your own word to make a Litany.

Rainbow

Practise reading the poem aloud. It has: a strong rhythm
repetition
a sense of humour

Try to bring all these out as you read it.

On my island

Congratulations!

Operation Island Survival

You have been selected as one of a small group of people your age to take part in Operation Island Survival. For one month you and your companions will live together on an uninhabited island to show just how resourceful, brave and fit the young people of this country are. You will make decisions, have adventures and then describe the things that happen to you.

You have the chance to decide which of these three islands your group will live on.

1. Study all the information carefully.
2. For each island make two lists: one of the good points; the other of the bad points.
3. Look at your lists and decide which of the islands you think the team should choose.
4. Write a short explanation of why you have chosen that island.
5. Now think about what the whole island is like and draw a map showing its main features. Use the information on these pages and add other details of your own.

Burion island

Travel to the deserted island of Burion and you will enter a tropical paradise. The island boasts an abundance of wild life – you will see animals, birds and fish that you have never dreamed of in a setting of luxurious vegetation. But beware! All is not as it seems. Many of the animals are hostile to humans: for example, poisonous snakes and fierce mountain cats. Many of the exotic fruits may provide a wonderful meal for the traveller, but some contain a deadly poison. And – to cap it all – there is no source of drinking water on the island – unless you are clever enough to find some way of catching and storing the rain when it falls, which it does almost every day.

Some of the 'friendlier' inhabitants of Burion island.

Captain Ferguson and his companions found that storms like this were common on Clovis island.

We spent ten days on the island and found it a place of contrasts. In general it was pleasantly cool, and there were no problems in finding water to drink and food to eat. (But only vegetables – there seemed to be no animals we could catch to provide meat, and we had no luck when we tried to fish.) It is heavily wooded and this, combined with the frequent heavy rains which sweep the island, makes it a rather gloomy place to live. Also it can be very cold at night, and we were forced to make ourselves strong and comfortable huts in which to live.

Clovis island

Apoa island

The island is low and risks severe flooding at times of high tides or storms. While the climate is always warm and dry, this can cause problems. There is only one stream and in periods when the rains fail this can dry up altogether. Vegetation is thus rather scarce. The only food easily gathered is the coconut. Fish are plentiful, but it is necessary to travel some hundreds of yards from the shore to catch them, because the waters close in are so shallow.

Apoa island overwhelmed by hurricane Brian.

Travelling companions

NATHAN FELECCIA
aged 13

Strong and athletic: a keep-fit freak. Independent and inclined to want to do things on his own without help from anyone. Has a phobia about snakes.

JULYARA KHAN
aged 12

Efficient, sensible and hard-working. Has very firm views of her own on most subjects, and she can be impatient with people who do not see things her way. Vegetarian.

CRAIG WINSTANLEY
aged 11

Not physically strong but easy-going: he is always a very popular member of any group he is in. He loves cooking and he is very good at it. Suffers from asthma.

PAULINE THOMAS
aged 13

She's active and fit: one of her school's best football players. She is also good at practical things and regularly comes top in Craft Design and Technology. Hates all domestic tasks. Only eats junk food.

SHELAGH VINE
aged 12

Helpful, willing and chatty: she is very good at cheering people up when they are low. Can be disorganised and untidy. She is not a natural leader and does not like to be in charge. Short-sighted.

You have been asked to choose two extra people to join the group who will live on the island. These five have been suggested.

1   For each person decide what are their strong points and what are their weak points as members of the Island Survival team.
2   Decide which two you would choose and why.
3   Now write a short description of yourself which sums up your strong and weak points in the same way as the descriptions on this page.

Equipment

Before you are left on the island, you are allowed to choose some equipment: six necessities and two luxuries. For everything shown, there is a sufficient supply for all the members of the group.

It is the day before you leave. You know who your companions will be; you know what equipment you are taking; you know quite a lot about the island. Write your diary entry describing how you feel as you prepare to leave for the island.

1 Decide on your six necessities. Write them down and explain why you have chosen them.
2 Write down your two luxuries and explain why you have chosen them.
3 Every member of the group has to keep a diary in which they describe their experiences and how they feel about them.
4 Now write a second diary entry in which you describe what happens as you arrive on the island. Describe what happens, but also how you and other members of the group feel about arriving, and how you feel as you see the ship that brought you gradually disappearing again.

Living on the island

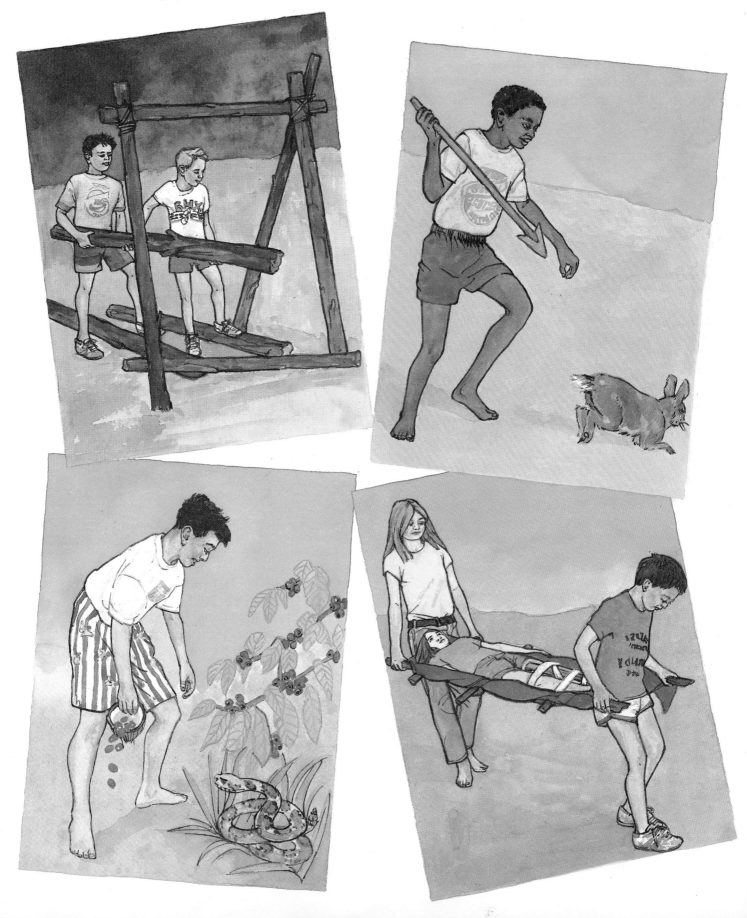

1 Think about what your group will have to do if they are to survive on the island. Remember the information you have about your chosen island and the members of your group. Look at the pictures on this page: they should give you some ideas, but you should also think of your own.

2 Make a list of the main things your group will have to do and the problems they will have to face.

3 Put them in order, with the most important at the top, and those which are less important lower down.

4 For each of the things to be done and problems to be solved, work out the best approach. Write them down.

5 Now think about what actually happens as your group starts its life on the island – sometimes things go well; sometimes not so well. Write your diary for the first full day.

Problems

'What we need is another window.'
'No. The rain'll get in.'
'What we need is a better roof.'
'The walls aren't strong enough.'

'Why don't you give us a hand?'
'It's not my turn.'
'It's never your turn.'
'Yes it is. I did something... the day before yesterday.'

BUT I THOUGHT IT WAS MY TURN TO GET THE WOOD

'We've got plenty of wood, then.
Anybody brought any water?'

'Why don't you give him a hand?'
'Give him a hand yourself. I can't stand him.'

As you can see, things do not always turn out well. Look at the words and pictures on these two pages. Think about the human problems you might face on the island.

1 Choose one of the four pictures on page 94. Role play the whole conversation.
2 Now do the same for one of the other pictures on page 94.
3 Choose one of the two conversations you have just had and make a written version of it. Write it as a script. (See page 180 if you are not sure how to do this.)
4 Now look at each of those four pictures in turn. Think about each one and decide exactly what the problem is. For each picture, write down your explanation of the problem and how you think it should be solved.

5 Choose one of the four pictures. Imagine that it is a situation that you were involved in. Write your diary for that day.
6 In the picture above the children have decided to try to sort out their problems. You can see some of the things that people say. Make a list of the main problems they mention. What do you think they should do to solve them?
7 Think about how the whole debate might have gone. Now write a diary extract in which you describe what people said, what was decided, and your thoughts and feelings about it.

*B*ecky and the wheels-and-brakes boys

Even my own cousin Ben was there – riding away, in the ringing of bicycle bells down the road. Every time I came to watch them – see them riding round and round enjoying themselves – they scooted off like crazy on their bikes.

They can't keep doing that. They'll see!

I only want to be with Nat, Aldo, Jimmy and Ben. It's no fair reason they don't want to be with me. Anybody could go off their head for that. Anybody! A girl can not, not, let boys get away with it all the time.

Bother! I have to walk back home, alone.

I know total-total that if I had my own bike, the Wheels-and-brakes Boys wouldn't treat me like that. I'd just ride away with them, wouldn't I?

Over and over I told my mum I wanted a bike. Over and over she looked at me as if I was crazy. 'Becky, d'you think you're a boy? Eh? D'you think you're a boy? In any case, where's the money to come from? Eh?'

Of course I know I'm not a boy. Of course I know I'm not crazy. Of course I know all that's no reason why I can't have a bike. No reason! As soon as I get indoors I'll just have to ask again – ask Mum once more.

At home, indoors, I didn't ask my mum.

It was evening time, but sunshine was still big patches in yards and on housetops. My two younger brothers, Lenny and Vin, played marbles in the road. Mum was taking measurements of a boy I knew, for his new trousers and shirt. Mum made clothes for people. Meggie, my sister two years younger than me, was helping Mum on the verandah. Nobody would be pleased with me not helping. I began to help.

Granny-Liz would always stop fanning herself to drink up a glass of iced water. I gave my granny a glass of iced water, there in her rocking-chair. I looked in the kitchen to find shelled coconut pieces to cut into small cubes for the fowls' morning feed. But Granny-Liz had done it. I came and started tidying up bits and pieces of cut-off material around my mum on the floor. My sister got nasty, saying she was already helping Mum. Not a single good thing was happening for me.

With me even being all so thoughtful of Granny's need of a cool drink, she started up some botheration against me.

Listen to Granny-Liz: 'Becky, with you moving about me here on the verandah, I hope you don't have any centipedes or scorpions in a jam jar in your pocket.'

'No, mam,' I said sighing, trying to be calm. 'Granny-Liz,' I went on, 'you forgot. My centipede and scorpion died.' All the same, storm broke against me.

'Becky,' my mum said. 'You know I don't like you wandering off after dinner. Haven't I told you I don't want you keeping company with those awful riding-about bicycle boys? Eh?'

'Yes, mam.'

'Those boys are a menace. Riding bicycles on sidewalks and narrow paths together, ringing bicycle bells and braking at people's feet like wild bulls charging anybody, they're heading for trouble.'

'They're the Wheels-and-brakes Boys, mam.'

'The what.'

'The Wheels-and-brakes Boys.'

'Oh! Given themselves a name as well, have they? Well, Becky, answer this. How d'you always manage to look like you've just escaped from a hair-pulling battle? Eh? And don't I tell you not to break the back down and wear your canvas shoes like slippers? Don't you ever hear what I say?'

'Yes, mam.'

'D'you want to end up a field labourer? Like where your father used to be overseer?'

'No, mam.'

'Well, Becky, will you please go off and do your homework?'

Everybody did everything to stop me. I was allowed no chance whatsoever. No chance to talk to Mum about the bike I dream of day and night! And I knew exactly the bike I wanted. I wanted a bike like Ben's bike. Oh, I wished I still had even my scorpion on a string to run up and down somebody's back!

I answered my mum. 'Yes, mam.' I went off into Meg's and my bedroom.

I sat down at the little table, as well I might. Could homework stay in anybody's head in broad daylight outside? No. Could I keep a bike like Ben's out of my head? Not one bit. That bike took me all over the place. My beautiful bike jumped every log, every rock, every fence. My beautiful bike did everything cleverer than a clever cowboy's horse, with me in the saddle. And the bell, the bell was such a glorious gong of a ring!

If Dad was alive I could talk to him. If Dad was alive he'd give me money for the bike like a shot.

I sighed. It was amazing what a sigh could do. I sighed and tumbled on a great idea. Tomorrow evening I'd get Shirnette to come with me.

Both of us together would be sure to get the boys interested to teach us to ride. Wow! With Shirnette they can't just ride away!

Next day at school everything went sour. For the first time, Shirnette and me had a real fight, because of what I hated most.

Shirnette brought a cockroach to school in a shoe-polish tin. At playtime she opened the tin and let the cockroach fly into my blouse. Pure panic and disgust nearly killed me. I crushed up the cockroach in my clothes and practically ripped my blouse off, there in open sunlight.

98

Oh the smell of a cockroach is the nastiest ever to block your nose! I started running with my blouse to go and wash it. Twice I had to stop and be sick.

I washed away the crushed cockroach stain from my blouse. Then the stupid Shirnette had to come into the toilet, falling about laughing. All right, I knew the cockroach treatment was for the time when I made my centipede on a string crawl up Shirnette's back. But you put fair-is-fair aside. I just barged into Shirnette.

When it was all over I had on a wet blouse, but Shirnette had one on too.

Then going home with the noisy flock of children from school I had ever such new, new idea. If Mum thought I was scruffy, Nat, Aldo, Jimmy and Ben might think so too. I didn't like that.

After dinner, I combed my hair in the bedroom. Mum did her machining on the verandah. Meggie helped Mum. Granny sat there, wishing she could take on any job, as usual.

I told Mum I was going to make up a quarrel with Shirnette. I went, but my friend wouldn't speak to me, let alone come out to keep me company. I stood alone and watched the Wheels-and-brakes Boys again.

This time the boys didn't race away past me. I stood leaning against the tall coconut palm tree. People passed up and down. The nearby main road was busy with traffic. But I didn't mind. I watched the boys. Riding round and round the big Flame-tree, Nat, Aldo, Jimmy and Ben looked marvellous.

At first each boy rode round the tree alone. Then each boy raced each other round the tree, going round three times. As he won, the winner rang his bell on and on, till he stopped panting and could laugh and talk properly. Next, most reckless and fierce, all the boys raced against each other. And, leaning against their bicycles, talking and joking, the boys popped soft drinks open, drank and ate chipped bananas.

I walked up to Nat, Aldo, Jimmy and Ben and said, 'Can somebody teach me to ride?'

'Why don't you stay indoors and learn to cook and sew and wash clothes?' Jimmy said.

I grinned. 'I know all that already,' I said. 'And one day perhaps I'll even be mum to a boy child, like all of you. Can you cook and sew and wash clothes, Jimmy? All I want is to learn to ride. I want you to teach me.'

I didn't know why I said what I said. But everybody went silent and serious.

One after the other, Nat, Aldo, Jimmy and Ben got on to their bikes and rode off. I wasn't at all cross with them. I knew they'd be heading into the town to have ice-cream and things and talk and laugh.

Mum was sitting alone on the verandah. She sewed buttons on to a white shirt she'd made. I sat down next to Mum. Straightaway, 'Mum,' I said, 'I still want to have a bike badly.'

'Oh, Becky, you still have that foolishness in your head? What am I going to do?'

Mum talked with some sympathy. Mum knew I was honest. 'I can't get rid of it, mam,' I said.

Mum stopped sewing. 'Becky,' she said, staring in my face, 'how many girls around here do you see with bicycles?'

'Janice Gordon has a bike,' I reminded her.

'Janice Gordon's dad has acres and acres of coconuts and bananas, with a business in the town as well.'

I knew Mum was just about to give in. Then my granny had to come out on to the verandah and interfere. Listen to that Granny-Liz. 'Becky, I heard your mother tell you over and over she can't afford to buy you a bike. Yet you keep on and on. Child, you're a girl.'

'But I don't want a bike because I'm a girl.'

'D'you want it because you feel like a boy?' Granny said.

'No. I only want a bike because I want it and want it and want it.'

Granny just carried on. 'A tomboy's like a whistling woman and a crowing hen, who can only come to a bad end. D'you understand?'

I didn't want to understand. I knew Granny's speech was an awful speech. I went and sat down with Lenny and Vin, who were making a kite.

By Saturday morning I felt real sorry for Mum. I could see Mum really had it hard for money. I had to try and help. I knew anything of Dad's - anything - would be worth a great mighty hundred dollars.

I found myself in the centre of town, going through the busy Saturday crowd. I hoped Mum wouldn't be too cross. I went into the fire station. With lots of luck I came face to face with a round face man in uniform. He talked to me. 'Little miss, can I help you?'

I told him I'd like to talk to the head man. He took me into the office and gave me a chair. I sat down. I opened out my brown paper parcel. I showed him my dad's sun helmet. I told him I thought it would make a good fireman's hat. I wanted to sell the helmet for some money towards a bike, I told him.

The fireman laughed a lot. I began to laugh too. The fireman put me in a car and drove me back home.

Mum's eyes popped to see me bringing home the fireman. The round face fireman laughed at my adventure. Mum laughed too, which was really good. The fireman gave Mum my dad's hat back. Then, mystery, mystery, Mum sent me outside while they talked.

My mum was only a little cross with me. Then - mystery and more mystery - my mum took me with the fireman in his car to his house.

The fireman brought out what? A bicycle! A beautiful, shining bicycle! His nephew's bike. His nephew had been taken away, all the way to America. The bike had been left with the fireman-uncle for him to sell it. And the good kind fireman-uncle decided we could have the bike - on small payments. My mum looked uncertain. But, in a big, big way the fireman knew it was all right. My mum took the bike from the fireman Mister Dean.

And guess what? Seeing my bike much, much newer than his, my cousin Ben's eyes popped with envy. But - he took on the big job. He taught me to ride. Then he taught Shirnette.

I ride into town with the Wheels-and-brakes Boys now. When she can borrow a bike, Shirnette comes too. We all sit together. We have patties and ice-cream and drink drinks together. We talk and joke. We ride about, all over the place.

And, again, guess what? Fireman Mister Dean became our best friend, and Mum's especially. He started coming round almost every day.

James Berry

Ant's pants

Characters
Anthony (12 year old boy)
Marlon (12 year old boy)
Fatty (12 year old girl)
Louise (12 year old girl)

(**Anthony** *and* **Marlon** *enter. They are in the centre of town.* **Marlon** *is obviously very bored.*)

Marlon: Why did we have to come shopping?

Ant: Because I need a new shirt for the school disco on Friday.

Marlon: You're not going to that, are you?

Ant: Why not?

Marlon: It's rubbish! All the teachers bouncing about in their flower-power gear, trying to get you to dance with them, and old Fungus Williams playing his ancient records. 'Do-wah-diddy-diddy-dum-diddy-do.' It's pathetic!

Ant: You don't like school discos 'cos your mum turned up at the last one at nine o'clock to take you home, and Fungus announced it over the mike.

Marlon: Yeah, well it was embarrassing.

Ant: Anyway, I'm going. I've been practising this mega dance routine. Everybody is going to be well impressed!

Marlon: Bighead!

Ant: Oh, yeah? Watch this!

Marlon: Not here, Ant. You'll show me up!

Ant: Stand back and marvel!

(**Ant** *begins to hum one of the latest hit sounds and starts to move in time to it. His dancing gets wilder and wilder.*)

Ant: And now for the best bit!

(*He leaps up in the air and comes down in the 'splits' position. There is a loud ripping noise.*)

Ant: Oh no!

Marlon: What's the matter?

Ant: I've split my jeans!

Marlon: (*Bursting into laughter*) Serves you right, you bighead!

Ant: Don't just stand there, do something!

Marlon: Like what?

Ant: Get me something to cover it up.

Marlon: I haven't got anything. I've only got my T-shirt and you're not having that. You'll have to walk home like that.

Ant: I can't.

Marlon: Why not?

Ant: Promise you won't laugh.

Marlon: What at?

Ant: Just promise.

Marlon: OK

(**Ant** *whispers in* **Marlon**'s *ear.* **Marlon** *bursts into screams of laughter.*)

Ant: You promised!

Marlon: You're joking, aren't you? Let's have a look.

(**Marlon** *tries to look at* **Ant**'s *backside.* **Ant** *has now backed up against a wall.*)

Ant: Get lost!

Marlon: Whooooooo! You haven't, have you?

Ant: There weren't any in my cupboard and you came before I was ready...

Marlon: Hey, we can't call you Ant, anymore; we'll have to call you Nicholas. Knickerless, get it?

(**Marlon** *howls with laughter.*)

Ant: Stop making stupid jokes and do something!

Marlon: All right, all right. Hey, you could buy some new trousers.

Ant: I've only got enough for a shirt.

Marlon: Ah.

Ant: Come on, think! There's a terrible draught around here!

Marlon: I've got it! Give me ten pence.

Ant: What for?

Marlon: Do you want to get home or not?

Ant: OK. Here.

(**Ant** *gives* **Marlon** *ten pence.*)

Marlon: Stay here. Don't move.

(**Marlon** *runs off.*)

Ant: Hey! Where are you going? Marlon! Oh no! I'll probably get arrested for looking suspicious. They'll think I'm waiting to rob a bank or something. Where's he gone?

(**Marlon** *rushes back.*)

Marlon: Here you are.

(**Marlon** *hands* **Ant** *a black plastic bin-liner.*)

Ant: What's this?

Marlon: A bin-liner.

Ant: A bin-liner!

Marlon: Yeah. A liner. For bins.

Ant: You don't think I'm going to wear this, do you?

Marlon: Why not? Put a couple of holes in it for the legs. You'll be fine.

Ant: I'll look like a big baby wearing a big plastic nappy!

Marlon: If you're not happy, sort it out yourself.

Ant: Look, why don't you nip home and get me a pair of your trousers?

Marlon: Mine won't fit you.

Ant: Get your tracksuit bottoms then. They'll fit me.

Marlon: All right. You stay here and put the bin-liner on. Then you can move about a bit.

Ant: OK. Just hurry up then.

(**Marlon** *goes.* **Ant** *makes two holes in the bin-liner and starts to put it on.*)

Ant: This is ridiculous. This is the most embarrassing thing that's ever happened to me. Well, at least things can't get any worse.

(**Fatty** *and* **Louise** *appear.*)

Ant: I was wrong, they can.

104

Fatty: Hi, Ant!

Ant: Oh, hi, Fatty. Hello Louise. Are you all right?

Louise: We are, how about you?

Ant: Me? Oh, I'm fine.

Louise: Are you sure?

Ant: Of course.

Fatty: If you're all right, Ant, then why are you wearing a bin-liner?

Ant: Er, because er, that is... (**Ant** *is suddenly hit by a brainwave*) Don't you know?

Louise: Know what?

Ant: Why I'm wearing a bin-liner? I mean, you look as though you've never seen anyone wearing a bin-liner before.

Fatty: That's because we haven't.

Ant: Ah, but you will!

Louise: Why?

Ant: I'm surprised you haven't heard already. I thought you were up with the latest fashions.

Fatty: What are you on about?

Ant: Scum!

Fatty: There's no need to be like that!

Ant: They're a rock band, dummy.

Louise: I've never heard of them.

Fatty: Neither have I.

Ant: That's because they're from America. I saw them on telly at my mate's house. He's got satellite TV and they show all the latest trends first and the latest is 'Scum'.

Fatty: OK, so what do they do?

Ant: They wear rubbish!

Louise: Rubbish?

Ant: Yeah. They think that all designer label clothes are just expensive rip-offs. So they wear rubbish as a protest.

Louise: He's kidding us.

Fatty: What sort of rubbish?

Ant: Anything - potato sacks, vacuum cleaner bags, crisp packets...

Louise: That's stupid. You're lying.

Ant: If I'm lying, then why am I wearing a bin-liner? I'm letting you in on the latest fashion and all you can do is accuse me of lying.

Fatty: He's got a point, Louise. Hey, we could get one up on snobby Ursula. She's always reading the fashion mags and spends loads of money on clothes. We could beat her to this one...

Louise: But it's daft!

Ant: Most fashions are.

Fatty: Oh come on Louise.

Louise: OK then. Where did you get it?

Ant: The hardware shop round the corner, it was dead cheap.

Fatty: Great! Let's get one. Come on Louise.

(**Fatty** and **Louise** go. **Ant** grins. **Marlon** returns.)

Ant: You took your time.

Marlon: Well thanks a lot! Do you know how far it is to my house from here?

Ant: OK, OK, look Marlon...

Marlon: It's miles. I'm shattered. I ran all the way there and back.

Ant: All right, I'm sorry. Look...

Marlon: And all you can do is moan. I should have left you to look like a wally.

Ant: Will you shut up and listen?

(**Fatty** and **Louise** come back wearing their bin-liners.)

Fatty: Hi Marlon!

Louise: Here we are!

Marlon: What's going on? Have you done it too?

Louise: Done what?

Fatty: What are you going on about, Marlon?

Ant: Nothing! Come on Marlon...

Louise: What do you think then?

(**Louise** 'models' the bin-liner.)

Ant: Er, very nice...Well, time we were off. Come on Marlon!

Marlon: (*To the* **girls**) Were you dancing too?

Louise: (*Confused*) When?

Marlon: When you split your jeans.

Ant: Marlon, shut up!

Fatty: We haven't split our jeans.

Louise: Just a minute. Has he split his jeans? (*She points at* **Ant**.)

Marlon: Yeah. That's why he's wearing a bin-liner.

106

Louise: (*To* **Ant**) So there isn't a band called 'Scum'?

Ant: There might be...

Louise: And they don't wear rubbish?

Ant: They might do...

Louise: You liar!

Fatty: We could have turned up to the disco in these!

Louise: Ursula would have laughed her head off. That's the last time I listen to you.

Marlon: You mean to say that he talked you into wearing those things? Hey, listen. Do you know why he's wearing one?

Ant: Shut up, Marlon.

Marlon: Guess what he forgot this morning.

Ant: I'm warning you!

(**Marlon** *whispers in the* **girls**' *ears. They start laughing.*)

Fatty: He never!

Marlon: He did!

Louise: What a dope!

Ant: All right, don't go on about it. Marlon just give me the tracksuit bottoms.

Marlon: I can't. They're in the wash. These are all I could get. They were my grandads!

(**Marlon** *produces a pair of moth eaten, knee length, khaki green shorts. They look disgusting!*)

Ant: I can't go home in those! I'd look stupid. Everybody will laugh.

(**Louise** *takes the shorts from* **Marlon** *and throws them at* **Ant**.)

Louise: Well, you'll just have to tell them it's a new fashion!

(**Fatty, Louise** *and* **Marlon** *walk away laughing leaving* **Ant** *wearing the bin-liner and holding the shorts.*)

Steve Skidmore and *Steve Barlow*

Becky and the wheels-and-brakes boys

Thinking about the story

Think about these points in the story and then discuss them with other people.

1   What do Becky's family, and all the boys, think about girls and how they should behave ?
2   What does Becky think about this ?
3   What do you think about it ?

Thinking about the characters

What impression did you get of each of these people in the story ?

Becky
Shirnette
Mother
Granny-Liz

Becky's diary

Suppose Becky kept a diary. What would she write in it for the week in which she visited the fire station? Think about this, and then write the diary as if you were Becky.

Writing a story

1   This story contains other stories, which we can only guess at. For example, the scene in which Becky shows her new bike to Nat, Aldo, Jimmy and Ben. What do you think happens? Tell the story of it yourself.
2   Write a story in which parents treat you in a way that you believe to be unfair. This might be because of what they say you are or because of what they say that some of your friends are, particularly if they do not approve of them.

Ant's pants

Thinking about the play

Ant is very embarrassed at ripping his jeans. Marlon had been embarrassed by his mum coming to pick him up from the school disco.

1 What embarrassing things have happened to you?
2 How did you feel?
3 What did other people say to you?

Ant is showing off when he splits his trousers.

4 Do you think that he gets what he deserves?
5 Have you ever been showing off and something has happened to you?
6 Why do you think we like it when people who are being bigheaded get shown up?

Role play: Excuses

Thinking

There are many reasons why we tell lies. Here are some:

> To get out of trouble
> To get someone else out of trouble
> To make us look better than we are

Try to think of some more.

Situation: A parent is very angry because their son or daughter has arrived home late. The child has to 'explain' things.

> **Role A:** the mother or father.
> Think about why you are so angry.
> **Role B:** the son or daughter.
> Think about why you are late and the excuses you will give.

Starter: A says, 'Oh there you are. Where on earth have you been?'

Talking points: How convincing was **B**'s story? Did **A** believe it?

Return match

Now swop over roles: The **B**s are the parents and the **A**s are the children.
Can you think of any more situations that you might have to use an excuse? Try out some of these ideas.

Why were you...?

In pairs again. Label yourselves **A** and **B**.
As have to place **B**s in an embarrassing situation by asking them a question beginning with the words, 'Why were you...?'

For example:
A: Why were you sitting in the town hall fountain, with a goldfish bowl over your head?
It is then up to **B**s to give a reasonable excuse.
After two minutes, swop over the roles.

Marlon & co

Marlon : Sugden Avenue? That's where all the snobs live — in all those big houses. D'you have servants too?

Anthony : Don't be stupid, of course we don't. And we aren't snobs, either. (*He turns to look at* **Fateha**) Where do you live, er...

Fateha : Fateha.

Anthony : Fatty what?

Fateha : (*Embarrassed*) My name is Fateha.

Anthony : I bet people call you Fatty, don't they?

Fateha : (*Even more embarrassed*) No! They don't... well, not often, anyway...

Louise : Leave her alone 'Anthony'.

Anthony : My name's Ant — only my mother calls me Anthony.

Louise : Yes, well her name's Fateha, so don't call her Fatty.

Marlon : Hey you lot, we're supposed to be finding out about each other. Not having a slanging match. Where do you live, Fateha?

Fateha : In a flat in Chatterton Street, right in the centre of town. How about you, Louise. Where's Maltside?

Louise : It's a village about two and a half miles out of town.

Anthony : My last teacher used to go really mad if we talked about miles. (*Mimicking*) This country has been metric since before you were born. It's not two and a half miles, it's four centimetres.

Marlon : Kilometres you idiot.

Anthony : So now we all know where everyone lives. What do we do now?

Fateha : She said find out as much as we could–

Louise : –in five minutes. Anyone been timing?

Marlon : Yes, we've got another two minutes. Let's take it in turn to tell each other about our families, our interests and hobbies and things like that. Half a minute each.

Anthony : All right. You time us. Half a minute's not very long. I'll go fast, I mean first. (*He starts speaking very quickly and running all his words together.*) Ilivewithmyparentsandmylittlesistershe'sonly threeandshe'sareal–

Louise : Well if you're just going to mess about–

Fateha : I can't understand a word you're saying.

Anthony : Oh all right. (*Starts to speak very very slowly*) I - l - i - v - e - w - i - t - h - m - y - p - a - r - e - n - t - s

Marlon : This is stupid. (*Speaking to* **Fateha** *and* **Louise**) Let's just pretend he isn't here and get on with it on our own. You start Louise.

Louise : OK. My Dad works on a farm in Maltside, and we live in a cottage that belongs to the farmer. It's quite big, so me and my two sisters have all got our own rooms. They're both crazy about animals and they've got their own dogs. I'm not very interested in all that. I prefer sports – specially athletics and swimming. I like playing football, too, but they wouldn't let me play in the village under-12 team because I'm a girl.

Fateha : That's stupid.

Louise : That's what I said, but it didn't make them change their minds.

Marlon : Right. Now it's your turn Fateha.

Fateha : Like I said, we live in a flat in Chatterton Street. That's my father and mother and my brother and my sister. I share a room with my sister. She's fourteen and all she's interested in is clothes. I like making things. At the moment it's marionettes –

Louise : Marionettes?

Fateha : Yes – you know puppets – the sort that hang on strings.

Louise : Oh I see.

Fateha : Right Marlon. Now it's your turn.

Marlon : OK. We live in a flat, too. But it's not a block of flats – it's more like half an ordinary house. We live downstairs and there's an old lady called Mrs Parker who lives upstairs. There are only two bedrooms, so I have to share with Peter – he's my brother. He's only six and he's a Lego freak. There's Lego all over the place. I like animals. I've got two gerbils and a hamster. That's all, really.

Louise : Right. That's everyone. We've finished.

Anthony : Hey – what about me?

Marlon : You don't count.

Anthony : That's not fair.

Louise : You should have thought of that before you started fooling around.

Discussion

1 Do you think that Fateha, Louise and Marlon were fair to Anthony?
2 What are your reasons?
3 What would you have done if you had been them?
4 What would you have done if you were him?
5 What is your impression of each of the four of them? What gives you this impression?
6 The teacher set them to do something in a short time. How successful do you think they have been?

Writing

Choose one of the four. Write a description of the person you have chosen.

1 Start by collecting information about:
   ● their personality
   ● what they look like
   ● their home and family
2 Then write your description.

111

Morton carnival

Every summer Morton has a carnival. These pictures show some of the things that happened when Fateha, Louise, Anthony and Marlon went to the carnival.

If you look carefully at the pictures, you will see each of the four children more than once, but they don't all appear in all the pictures. Choose one of the four and try to work out what he or she must have been doing at each stage of the carnival. (For example, one of the pictures shows Marlon playing in the band. What was Fateha doing at that moment?)

For your chosen character, make a list of what they were:
● doing
● thinking
● feeling (what they could see, hear, taste, smell, and touch and also if they were happy, sad, excited, bored, or...)

Now write a description of 'What I did at the carnival'. (Write as if you were the person you have chosen.)

113

Whooo-ooo Flupper !

This world is called Positos VI PH. Wow, how I used to hate it!

'We're prisoners!' I'd shout. 'Never allowed out of this crummy unit!'

'And if we did get out, what would we do?' squeaked Lollo, my sister. She even waved her fists, which was pretty useless as she's only nine and small for her age. I'm nearly twelve.

We stared out of the unit's window. What did we see? A sort of grey-green blancmange, with some dirty yellow prehistoric-looking trees sticking out. And that's all.

'I hate you,' muttered Lollo.

I said nothing. What was there to say about Positos VI PH? The name tells you everything. The 'VI' means it's a sixth-order world – the smallest sort, the dregs. The 'PH' means 'partly hostile'. In other words, it has a tendency to kill humans. Charming.

'Let's play with the video,' I said.

'I'm sick of the video.'

'Chess, then.'

'You'll only win.' She chewed her lower lip for some time, then said, 'I'm going out.'

'You're not! It's not allowed!'

'I'm going out,' she repeated. I tried to stop her but she kept on putting on more and more outside gear. Even her helmet, although Positos air is breathable. Thick and muggy and smelly, but breathable.

I found myself doing what she was doing – donning boots, suit, bleeper and three sorts of weapon. It's no good arguing with Lollo. Anyhow, I'm supposed to take care of her. Big brother.

'We're off,' she said. Off we went. We followed the tracks of our parents' Ruff-stuff at first – the wide, deep tracks of its go-anywhere wheels. Mum and Dad are prospectors. They keep searching for something – anything – to sell back home, on Earth. It's a hard way to make a living.

The Ruff-stuff's tracks swept off to the right so we kept walking to the left. We didn't want to meet them. We'd get told off. After a time, I said, 'Look, Lollo, that's enough. Let's go home.' But she just marched on.

We came to the swamp.

Today, it's known as Lolly's Lagoon because she saw it first. 'Lagoon' is a bit grand: it's really just a big old swamp, surrounded by droopy trees with their roots half in and half out of the water. And big mossy, fungus-like growths here and there on the shores. We stood and looked at it. Lollo made a face. I broke off a piece of wood or whatever it is from a tree, if that's a tree, and flung it at one of the huge pancake things like giant water-lily leaves that floated on the surface of the water. There was a damp plaff! as the soggy wood hit the soggy pancake. 'Good shot!' I was about to say when it moved! It rose! It reared up! It sort of humped up in the middle, sucking water with it, shrugging sprays of water from its wavy edges! It was alive!

It took off! Its fringe, its edges, became folded-over hydroplanes. The humped-up middle part was clear of the water. It made an upside-down U shape. Its fringes rippled and it moved. I mean, really moved. I fell over backwards in the slimy mud.

At first it just zoomed along, hydro-planing. But it had another trick up its sleeves. Suddenly the water inside the hollow of the U seemed to boil. Somewhere inside itself, the thing had a sort of jet propulsion.

Now it didn't just move. It accelerated like one of those old twentieth century water-speed record breakers and hurtled over the water! It swept round in a huge curve. Lollo's mouth hung open. I gaped. It went so fast, we couldn't believe it. Then hiss! – surge! – vroom! – it headed straight for us like a thousand-miles-an-hour nightmare!

Now we were both on our backsides in the mud. But just as we thought it was going to flatten us, it somehow back-pedalled, slowed, cut its jets, rippled its fringes and turned pink. We stared at it and it seemed to stare at us.

Silence. Then the thing said, 'Whooo.'

Lollo whooed right back at it. I added a shaky whoo of my own.

The thing – it must have been five metres across – rippled its flanges invitingly and eased right to where we stood. It said, 'Whooo?'

You can guess what happened next. Lollo climbed aboard the thing. Her big brave brother followed. The thing said, 'Whooo!' and moved.

When we lived Earthside, Lollo and I tried everything: zeta-powered bikes, dune zoomers, no-grav gymnastics, the lot.

You can keep them all as long as you leave us Flupper.

Riding Flupper was Glory, Glory, Glory all the way. Not just the thrill of all that acceleration, all that speed, all that flying water. He was so nice about everything. He wanted us to be happy aboard him. He showed us the whole lagoon (it is very big), slowing down to let us see the most interesting parts, then hurtled off amid boiling clouds of spray to give us a thrill. He even realised that we might slide off him when he accelerated, and provided us with a vine, like a rope, to hang on to. He held on to the other end, it went underneath him.

Mum and Dad didn't find out about Flupper and us for more than a week. We faked the unit's video to show us 'in'. That was our only fear – being found out, being told 'No! Never again!' Meanwhile, Flupper showed us the deadly thorn bushes that wrap round their prey like octopuses: and then whooshed us off at savage speeds – sometimes so fast he aquaplaned over the water.

There were other Flupper-type lily pads, of course. They seemed to welcome us too. We called one the Clown because he used to follow Flupper, cutting him up and teasing him. All in fun, naturally. Flupper would pretend to skid and go out of control; it was terrific – we'd hang on like grim death to the rope.

We knew we were perfectly safe, of course. But we were wrong.

That day, we were on Flupper doing about a million miles an hour. The Clown was racing alongside and Lollo and I were showing off to him whooing and waving. Lollo raised one leg and waggled her foot cheekily. Her other foot slipped.

116

She fell down. The rushing water clutched at one of her legs. The pull of the water tore her off Flupper. For a second I glimpsed her wet, frightened face: then she was hurtling away from me, bouncing over the water like a rag doll, her arms and legs flailing.

She hit the blancmange of the shoreline, bounced over it and flew sprawling into some bushes. Poison thorn bushes.

She screamed. Loudly at first, then in an awful breathless sobbing way.

Flupper took me to the shore and I ran to Lollo. When I reached her, I stopped dead, appalled by what I saw. She was red, red all over. The thorns were cutting her to pieces. The bush wrapped itself tighter and tighter around her and the thorns kept going in.

Then the snake thing came. I had seen the snake things from a distance. This one had a prong like a dagger in its head. I was screaming at Flupper and dancing about in an agony of uselessness. I thought the snake thing wanted Lollo. It didn't. It dug its dagger into the roots of the bush. The bush was of a dirty purplish colour. As the dagger went in, the bush turned grey and all its thorns went pale and soft. It died almost instantly. Now the snake could go for Lollo.

But it was too slow, or too stupid: I just had time to grab her ankles and pull her away. I towed her over to the muddy shore and flung her aboard Flupper. I was yelling for Flupper to help, to do something, anything. But all he did was to leave the shore and head fast for another part of the lagoon, where the moulds and fungi overhang the water. I begged him not to, but he just went on, heading straight for them.

'Home, take me home!' I shouted to Flupper. He took no notice. I could say nothing to Lollo, she had become a silent, horrible, raw red thing. 'Not this way!' I shouted. 'Home!'

But still Flupper continued in the wrong direction, heading for the greyish clumps of mould and fungi. I hated those growths, they frightened me. And Flupper was not merely heading for them, he was in among them! 'No!' I screamed. But it was too late: the sticky greyish growths were brushing over Lollo's body, clinging to her, damply caressing her, sticking to her in wisps and clusters.'

And Flupper had done this deliberately! I lay down on him and beat at him with my fists. I must have been out of my mind...

Suddenly it didn't matter any more. I lay there, head buried in my arms, knowing that Lollo was dead: I would spend the rest of my life cursing myself and Flupper. Cursing and weeping.'

Then Lollo's voice said, close to my ear, 'Yuck! I am filthy! All bloody!'

I sat up and she was kneeling beside me, picking at herself disgustedly, trying to get rid of the fungi and moulds. And – unbelievably – as I watched, the cuts and stabs in her flesh healed.

'All this blood,' she said, in just the same voice she'd have used if she'd spotted chocolate round my mouth. 'How disgusting! You'll have to get it off. I can't.'

Later, I helped her sponge off the caked blood. It took a long time, there was so much of it. We did it at home back at the unit. We never got rid of the stains on her gear. Those stains gave us away, of course. Dad spotted them and Mum tore us apart. A real tongue-lashing. Almost as bad as the thorn bush, Lollo said.

Our parents wouldn't believe a word we said, so we took them to see Flupper. Dad carried a Trans Vox so that we could talk properly with him. I'm amazed that Lollo and I never thought of using the Trans Vox: it translates almost any language into our language. Soon, everyone was talking away like mad.

A little later – just a few months – we were rich. Rich as you can get!

All thanks to Flupper, of course. And those growths that used to frighten me, the moulds and fungi.

You know about penicillin? Alexander Fleming discovered it quite early in the twentieth century. The wonder antibiotic, the great cure-all. Well, our moulds and fungi (I mean Flupper's) turned out to be super penicillin, penicillin X 10,000. And Dad and Mum staked the claim so they have Galactic rights.

So we were and are everlastingly rich. 'Just think!' Mum said. 'We can go back to our proper home! Live Earthside!'

'I don't want to go back home!' Lollo said. 'I won't go, you can't make me go!'

Flupper, of course: she couldn't bear the thought of leaving him. I felt the same.

When we talked to Flupper about it, he said, 'Do you know how old I am?' We said no. 'I'm 245 Earth years old,' he said. 'And I've got another 150 to go...'

So perhaps Lollo and I won't make so much fuss about going back to Earth. We can always come back. And Flupper will always be there.

'Whooo-ooo, Flupper!'

Nicholas Fisk

The song of tyrannosaurus rex

I'm a rock, I'm a mountain, I'm a hammer and a nail
I'm an army and a navy, I'm a force ten gale

I'm a trooper, I'm a tearaway, and time will never see
Another king, or anything, that fights like me

I'm a sinner, I'm a winner, I'm a one-man government
I'm the will of the people, I'm the force that's never spent

I'm a business and a factory, the work-force and the boss
I'm the brains and the belly and I never make a loss

I'm a monumental mason and the gravestones that I make
Are carved of flesh and bone from the carcases I take

I'm a god, I'm a ghost, I'm the creak on the stair
I'm the grin that listens in when people say their prayers

I'm a crane, I'm a lorry, I'm a brand-new motorway
I set like concrete and I'm here to stay

O I'm big and I'm bad and I'm bold and I'm free
And the world will never see another villain like me

For I swagger and I swallow and the earth is my hotel
And I chew my meat in heaven and I lash my tail in hell!

William Scammell

The highwayman

Part One

The wind was a torrent of darkness among the gusty trees,
The moon was a ghostly galleon tossed upon cloudy seas,
The road was a ribbon of moonlight over the purple moor,
And the highwayman came riding–
      Riding – riding –
The highwayman came riding, up to the old inn-door.

He'd a French cocked-hat on his forehead, a bunch of lace at his chin
A coat of the claret velvet, and breeches of brown doe-skin:
They fitted with never a wrinkle; his boots were up to the thigh!
And he rode with a jewelled twinkle,
      His pistol butts a-twinkle,
His rapier hilt a-twinkle, under the jewelled sky.

Over the cobbles he clattered and clashed in the dark inn-yard,
And he tapped with his whip on the shutters, but all was locked and barred:
He whistled a tune to the window; and who should be waiting there
But the landlord's black-eyed daughter,
      Bess, the landlord's daughter,
Plaiting a dark red love-knot into her long black hair.

And dark in the dark old inn-yard a stable-wicket creaked
Where Tim, the ostler, listened; his face was white and peaked,
His eyes were hollows of madness, his hair like mouldy hay;
But he loved the landlord's daughter,
      The landlord's red-lipped daughter:
Dumb as a dog he listened, and he heard the robber say–

'One kiss, my bonny sweetheart, I'm after a prize tonight,
But I shall be back with the yellow gold before the morning light.
Yet if they press me sharply, and harry me through the day,
Then look for me by moonlight,
      Watch for me by moonlight:
I'll come to thee by moonlight, though Hell should bar the way.'

He rose upright in the stirrups, he scarce could reach her hand;
But she loosened her hair i'the casement! His face burnt like a brand
As the black cascade of perfume came tumbling over his breast;
And he kissed its waves in the moonlight,
      (Oh, sweet black waves in the moonlight)
Then he tugged at his reins in the moonlight, and galloped away to the West.

Part Two

He did not come in the dawning, he did not come at noon;
And out of the tawny sunset, before the rise o' the moon,
When the road was a gypsy's ribbon, looping the purple moor,
A red-coat troop came marching –
      Marching – marching –
King George's men came marching, up to the old inn-door.

They said no word to the landlord, they drank his ale instead;
But they gagged his daughter and bound her to the foot of her narrow bed.
Two of them knelt at her casement, with muskets at the side!
There was death at every window;
      And Hell at one dark window;
For Bess could see, through her casement, the road that *he* would ride.

They had tied her up to attention, with many a sniggering jest:
They had bound a musket beside her, with the barrel beneath her breast!
'Now keep good watch!' and they kissed her.
　　　She heard the dead man say –
Look for me by moonlight;
　　　Watch for me by moonlight;
I'll come to thee by moonlight, though Hell should bar the way!

She twisted her hands behind her; but all the knots held good!
She writhed her hands till her fingers were wet with sweat or blood!
They stretched and strained in the darkness, and the hours crawled by like years;
Till, now, on the stroke of midnight,
　　　Cold, on the stroke of midnight,
The tip of one finger touched it! The trigger at least was hers!

The tip of one finger touched it; she strove no more for the rest!
Up, she stood to attention, with the barrel beneath her breast,
She would not risk their hearing: she would not strive again;
For the road lay bare in the moonlight,
　　　Blank and bare in the moonlight;
And the blood of her veins in the moonlight throbbed to her Love's refrain.

Tlot-tlot, tlot-tlot! Had they heard it? The horse-hoofs ringing clear-
Tlot-tlot, tlot-tlot, in the distance? Were they deaf that they did not hear?
Down the ribbon of moonlight, over the brow of the hill,
The highwayman came riding, Riding, riding!
The red-coats looked to their priming! She stood up straight and still!

Tlot-tlot, in the frosty silence! *Tlot-tlot* in the echoing night!
Nearer he came and nearer! Her face was like a light!
Her eyes grew wide for a moment; she drew one last deep breath,
Then her finger moved in the moonlight,
      Her musket shattered the moonlight,
Shattered her breast in the moonlight and warned him - with her death.

He turned; he spurred him westward; he did not know who stood
Bowed with her head o'er the musket, drenched with her own red blood!
Not till the dawn he heard it, and slowly blanched to hear
How, Bess, the landlord's daughter,
      The landlord's black-eyed daughter,
Had watched for her Love in the moonlight; and died in the darkness there.

Back, he spurred like a madman, shrieking a curse to the sky,
With the white road smoking behind him, and his rapier brandished high!
Blood-red were his spurs i'the golden noon; wine-red was his velvet coat;
When they shot him down on the highway,
      Down like a dog on the highway,
And he lay in his blood on the highway, with the bunch of lace at his throat.

Part Three

And still of a winter's night, they say, when the wind is in the trees,
When the moon is a ghostly galleon tossed upon cloudy seas,
When the road is a ribbon of moonlight over the purple moor,
A highwayman comes riding –
      Riding – riding –
A highwaymen comes riding, up to the old inn-door.

Over the cobbles he clatters and clangs in the dark inn-yard;
And he taps with his whip on the shutters, but all is locked and barred:
He whistles a tune to the window, and who should be waiting there
But the landlord's black-eyed daughter,
      Bess, the landlord's daughter,
Plaiting a dark red love-knot into her long black hair.

Alfred Noyes

Whooo-ooo Flupper!

Thinking about the story

1 We see the whole of this story from the point of view of the boy: we see what he sees, feel what he feels and he tells us his thoughts. How did this affect your enjoyment of the story?

2 What would it have been like, if it had been told by his sister? Would she have told it in a different way? If so, how?

3 We are not told much about their parents - although we do learn a little. How do you think they felt about the children's adventures:

    a) immediately afterwards
    b) when they met Flupper
    c) when they found out about super penicillin?

Writing a different version

Like many stories, this one could be told in different versions. Choose one of these.

1 Tell the story from Lollo's point of view. Write as if you were Lollo.

2 Flupper meets the children's parents. Through the Trans Vox they are able to talk to each other. Flupper tells them its story: not just what happened, but also about what it is like to live on Positos VI PH. You can write it as a story told by Flupper, or as a conversation.

3 The children's parents tell their version of the story, starting at the moment when they see the stains on Lollo's gear, and going on to the point where they realise they (or their children) have discovered super penicillin.

The song of tyrannosaurus rex

Reading aloud

How do you think this poem should be read aloud?

Either
    a) work out how to read it on your own
Or
    b) plan a group reading with one or two other people.

Think about these things:

1 What is the main effect you want to have as you read the poem?
2 How can you vary the way in which you read it?
3 Which parts should be the loudest?
4 Are there any parts that should be quiet?
5 How should the speed vary as you read?

Comparisons

This poem describes tyrannosaurus rex, by using comparisons. Each one of them tells us about a different aspect of the creature. Pick out some of the comparisons that really helped you imagine what tyrannosaurus rex was like. Write each one down on a table like the one on the opposite page. Then write a sentence or two describing why you think it is a good comparison. It has been started to show you how to use it.

Comparison	Reason I chose it
I'm a force ten gale	A force ten gale is very powerful and frightening. It also makes a lot of noise - so it tells us these things about tyrannosaurus rex.

The highwayman

Reading Part One

On your own
1 Read the whole poem carefully to yourself.
2 Read Part One again. Make a list of any words or phrases whose meaning you are not too sure about. Use a dictionary to help you sort out the problems.
3 Write a few sentences to tell the story of what happens in Part One.

With a partner
4 Now read the poem with your partner. Divide the lines between you in any way which you think adds to the drama and suspense.

● Get the feel of the beat. Try tapping it out.
● Try reading at different speeds. Which is best?
● Make sure your voice does not fade.
● Sound the rhymes clearly.
● Try exaggerating the rhythm a little.
● Use a different voice for the lines spoken by the highwayman. (What kind of accent might he have?)
5 Practise reading Part One until you are happy with it.

Parts Two and Three

6 Do the same with the rest of the poem.
7 Read the whole poem together, right through. Practise it until you are happy with your reading and confident to read it to other people.

Part B

Using words

That reminds me

Remembering

The picture contains the beginnings of lots of true stories that people can remember about themselves. Choose one of the beginnings that reminds you of something that happened to you. Think about exactly what happened – try to remember all the details that make it vivid in your mind.

Telling

Now share your story with a partner.

1 Decide who will go first.
2 Tell your own story as vividly as you can.
3 Listen carefully to your partner's story.
4 Do the stories remind you of other true stories from your own life? If so, tell your partner those, too.

Writing

1 Choose one of the stories you told your partner.
2 Remember all the details that you can – you may have forgotten some of them when you were telling it the first time.
3 Write your story for your partner to read.

Reading

Work with the same partner as before.

1 Swap stories.
2 As you read your partner's story compare it with what you heard when the story was told aloud. What differences do you notice between the two versions?
3 Make a list of any differences you have noticed.
4 Discuss with your partner how the two stories have changed between telling them and writing them down. Why do you think they have changed?

128

Changes

When people make up stories, they often start from something that has really happened to them. Then they change things so that the final story is fiction.

Planning

1 Choose one of the stories you told last time.
2 Think of ways in which you could change it to make it really different:
  ● funnier
  ● more exciting or dramatic
  ● stranger
3 Think the story through in your head.

Telling

Now share your story with a partner.

1 Decide who will go first.
2 Tell your own story as vividly as you can.
3 Listen carefully to your partner's story.
4 Talk about the two stories – are there any ways in which they can be made even better?

Writing

Now write your story down. If you think of new ideas and details as you are writing, include them too.

Reading

Work with the same partner as before.

1 Swap stories.
2 As you read your partner's story compare it with what you heard when the story was told aloud. What differences do you notice between the two versions?
3 Make a list of any differences you have noticed.
4 Discuss with your partner how the two stories have changed between telling them and writing them down.

*R*ead me a story...

If you have got a younger brother or sister, you have probably heard that before now. It is useful to be able to read aloud well, not just to brothers and sisters, but to other people as well. This unit gives practice in reading aloud.

What makes a good reading?

Not everyone is good at reading aloud. It needs practice. These pictures show some of the things you have to think about when reading aloud.

130

▶ You will need a partner to work with. Some of the work is done on your own and some is done in pairs. All the activities have a number: do them in that order.

▶ Look at the pictures on the page opposite. Each one shows a problem about reading aloud.

1 What is the problem in each picture? Make a list of them.
2 Discuss your list with your partner.
3 Make a list of good advice for people who want to read aloud well.

Now you are going to read the story of *Mrs Sugar* below.

4 Read the story carefully.
5 Look at the list of good advice you made. Think about how you will read the story aloud so that your listener will find it interesting and amusing.
6 Read it again to yourself, and try to 'hear it in your head', as it should sound.
7 When you are both ready, decide who will be the first to read the story.
8 As your partner is reading, listen carefully. Remembering your list of good advice, make notes on the good and bad points in your partner's reading.
9 At the end of the reading tell your partner what you thought.
10 Now do the same for the other reading.

Mrs Sugar

I know this is a true story, because when my Aunt Peg was a little girl she used to live next door to Mrs Sugar, who was a witch. Mrs Sugar used to curl her hair with rags and take snuff, and every Saturday she had a bet on the horses. Everybody in the street knew she was a witch. She used to give you silverweed for freckles and camomile for bellyache.

Anyway, Mrs Sugar died, and she was buried in the cemetery, and had an angel on her grave. Soon after a story started going round that Mrs Sugar was still taking her usual walk out on Saturday evenings. I don't know how the story got started. Maybe people thought that since she'd been a witch when alive, she'd be a ghost once she was dead.

Most adults said the story was just a story, but most children believed it, and they used to go in gangs to the cemetery, especially on a Saturday night, and peer through the railings, trying to spot Mrs Sugar coming out. If a cat stuck its leg in the air, they all raced off, screaming that they'd seen something move. A lot of them said they'd seen Mrs Sugar, but none of them really had, and nobody believed them.

After weeks of this game, they got bored with Mrs Sugar, since she never turned up, no matter how long they watched for her. In fact, when my Aunt Peg got the idea to scare her friends, she'd forgotten all about Mrs Sugar...

The burnt book

Sandra: I tell you, I still don't believe I saw it.

Craig: You've said that three times now but you still haven't told me what it is. Shall I tell you what I saw in my old man's garden shed last summer? Serves him right for leaving it open.

Sandra: Wanny told me that months ago and I don't believe it any more than he does. There's not enough space in there.

Craig: You don't have to believe it. I do because I saw it.

Sandra: And I saw Cheryl Johnson.

Craig: Everyone's seen Cheryl Johnson. And heard her. With a mouth like that, she's not exactly going to fade into the background is she?

Sandra: She borrowed Shelima's book at the end of science. I only know because she tried to borrow mine to copy up but I'm always behind as well.

Craig: Cheryl's not so much always behind as all behind. That's why you can't miss her.

Sandra: Shut up and listen for once. I didn't use the toilets between lessons because I hate all that smoke so, by the time Biffo had finished with us, I dashed straight down to them. It was so late everyone had gone home except Cheryl. I thought for a second she was smoking so I avoided her and I don't think she noticed me. When I came out, there was Shelima's science book in a wash-basin smouldering away. The idiot had set fire to it.

Craig: So what did you do?

Sandra: I turned a tap on and damped it down. It's a bit of a mess but it's not totally destroyed.

Craig: How on earth are you going to give that back to Shelima? I can see it now: 'Hallo, Shelima, here's your science book. It's wet through and 75% burnt but I kept it for you.'

Sandra: I thought I might take it to Mr Wilson.

Craig: And what will you tell him?

Sandra: The truth.

Craig: It will be your word against hers. And then she'll take you apart bit by bit in this very park when all the teachers have slunk off home.

Sandra: I'm not scared of her. She's all mouth.

Craig: She also goes to judo and weight-training.

Sandra: Well what else can I do?

Craig: You can forget all about it.

Sandra: But Shelima's my friend.

Craig: She was Cheryl's friend as well and look what happened.

Sandra: Perhaps I could talk to Cheryl.

Craig: Perhaps you could just lose what's left of the book, forget about it.

Sandra: Craig Harding, you've got no feelings for others at all.

Craig: And you, Sandra Gibbons, have got no sense.

▶ What should Sandra do?

1 Copy and complete this table as fully as you can.

2 Look at what you have written. Decide what you would have done if you had been Sandra, and why.

Action	Advantages	Disadvantages
Nothing. Confront Cheryl Johnson about the burning of the book. Tell Shelima what happened. Find a way of telling a teacher. <u>My own ideas</u>:		

Where were you?

When you are talking to a teacher in school, you speak and act in a different way from when you are talking to your friends out of school. This is because you have a different *role*. In one case you are a pupil; in the second you are a friend. We all *play* different *roles* at different times. Most of the time we do not really think about this but sometimes it is interesting to see how our language changes according to the role we play. We can do this by setting up a *role play*.

Plain and simple

Situation: This is not really a role play, because both **A** and **B** just have to be themselves and tell the truth. **A** just has to find out in detail what **B** was doing yesterday evening between 6pm and 8pm.

Role A: The questioner.
Role B: The person being questioned.

Starter: **A** says, 'What did you do last night?'

Talking points: How much detail did **B** give? Did **A** have to ask a lot of questions? How did **A**'s questions help **B** tell the story?

What happened to you?

Situation: **A** and **B** are friends who had planned to meet at 6 o'clock last night to see a film. **A** turned up but **B** did not.

Role A: Decide how you feel about this: are you cross, disappointed, or what?
Role B: Keep the details of what you were doing the same as for the last interview. Decide why you did that rather than meeting **A**.

Starter: **A** says, 'Where were you last night?'

Talking points: **B** is providing the same information as before. How does it change in the telling?

Homework?

Situation: **A** is a teacher who told the class yesterday that an important piece of homework must be done that night. **B** has not got the homework.

Role A: Teacher. Decide how you feel about this.
Role B: Pupil. Keep the details of what you did last night the same. Decide why you did that rather than doing the homework.

Starter: **A** says, 'Where's that homework I set you?'

Talking points: How does **B**'s story, and the way it is told, change this time?

A serious matter

Situation: **A** is a police-officer investigating some damage that has been done near the school **A** thinks that **B** may have had something to do with it.

Role A: Police-officer. You have got to find out whether **B** is telling the truth or not.
Role B: Yourself. Tell the same story as before. This time, however, you know that it is not true. (Decide : where you were; what you were doing; why you aren't telling the truth.)

Starter: **A** says, 'Now then. Exactly what were you doing at 6 o'clock last night, eh?'

Talking points: How has **B**'s behaviour changed from last time? Does he/she give himself/herself away?

What to do

1 Deciding

Decide who is going to play each role. If necessary decide when and where the conversation takes place.

2 Preparing

1 Read the notes for your role.
2 Think about your role and how you will behave.
3 If you need to be sitting or standing in a particular way, sort this out.
4 Get ready to start.

3 Starting

Either
use the **Starter** sentence,
or
make up one of your own.

4 The interview

While you are having the conversation, *concentrate* :
- on what is being said
- on *staying in role* – being the person you are supposed to be
- on keeping your conversation realistic
- on not showing off

5 Talking it over

Talk about what happened. Use the **Talking points**, but also talk about things you think are important.

Join the group

A lot of the work you do in English and other subjects involves working in groups. This unit is about how to make your group work better. You will need to work in groups of three or four.

A problem

Marnie and George are brother and sister. Marnie is eleven and George is ten. They both get the same pocket-money each week. Their mother and father have told them that it is about time they started helping a bit more at home. This is what they have said:

Marnie 🎀	George 🎩
1. Keep bedroom clean and tidy, including making bed properly every day.	1. keep bedroom clean and tidy, including making bed properly every day.
2. Do the washing up after tea every day.	2. Clean the car once a week.
3. Give Mum a hand getting meals, if she asks.	3 Help Dad in the garden at weekends, if he asks.
NO HELP – NO POCKET MONEY	NO HELP – NO POCKET MONEY

1 Discuss the questions listed below.
2 Decide what you think as a group.
3 Make a note of what you agree.
4 Decide who will report back to the rest of the class what you have decided.

- Do you think what the parents have decided is fair?
- What are your reasons?
- If it is unfair, how should it be changed and why?

Writing

On your own, write down your answers to these questions.

1 Do you think your group produced the best answer to the problem?
2 Did you get a fair chance to express your opinion? (Or did you feel that you wanted to say more?)
3 Did everyone else get a fair chance to express their opinion? (Or were some people very quiet?)
4 Did people listen to what other people were saying?
5 Did everyone understand clearly what they had to do?
6 How did the group agree on its answer?
7 How did everyone feel about the answer that was agreed?
8 Was it an equal group, or did someone act as a boss?

Discussion

In your group, discuss everyone's answers to the questions.

Getting an agreement

In a good group:

1 Everyone listens to everyone else.
2 There is one good leader.
3 Everyone understands what is going on.
4 Everyone has a fair chance to speak.
5 There are no quarrels and arguments.
6 The group pauses every so often to check how they are getting on.
7 Decisions are made by agreeing, not by voting.
8 Everyone has a chance to be the leader.
9 The group plans how it is going to work before it starts.
10 People do not interrupt each other.

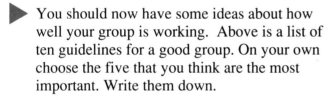 You should now have some ideas about how well your group is working. Above is a list of ten guidelines for a good group. On your own choose the five that you think are the most important. Write them down.

Discussion

In your group, discuss the guidelines. Choose the five that you as a group think are the most important. Make sure that everyone writes down the five you agree on.

Writing

On your own, look at the five guidelines you have written down. Did your group follow these guidelines while it was working? For each guideline answer the following two questions in the next colum and write down the marks your group scored.

Was this guideline followed:

1 Hardly any of the time?
2 Some of the time?
3 Most of the time?
4 All of the time?

Was the guideline followed by:

1 Hardly any of us?
2 Some of us?
3 Most of us?
4 All of us?

Discussion

Now discuss your results with the rest of your group. Decide:

1 Which guideline did you follow most closely?
2 Which guideline did you follow least successfully?
3 Which guidelines do you need to think about and work at?

*I*n the hot seat

Hot seating is a way of finding out more about the characters in stories, plays, improvisations or poems.

It can tell us:

● What sort of people the characters are
● Why they behave as they do
● What they are thinking

The best way of finding this information out would be to ask the characters themselves. Of course, it is impossible to ask questions of characters who do not really exist. Therefore, you, or other members of your group, have to become these characters and speak for them.

How to hot seat

1 Decide which character in the story you wish to question.
2 Choose one member of your group to play that character.
3 This person sits in a chair (the hot seat) facing the rest of the group.
4 As soon as s/he sits in the hot seat, this person must become the chosen character.
5 The group asks the character questions.
6 The person in the hot seat answers these questions as the character.

●● Tips ●●●●●●●●●●●●●●●●●●●●●

● Always address the person in the hot seat by the name of the character you have chosen.

● Ask your questions one at a time.

● Start with easy questions before asking more difficult ones. This will help the person in the hot seat to become more relaxed and confident in the role of the character.

How it works

When we are reading *Ant's pants* on page 102 we might want to know why Ant tries to trick Fatty and Louise instead of just telling the truth. We can put Ant in the hot seat to find out.

You try

Of course not every character has the same point of view. Would Louise and Fatty agree with what Ant has just said? Put them in the hot seat and question them to find out.

Create your own character

▶ The person in the picture is creating her own character.
She has answered all the group's questions.

1 Which answer matches which question?
2 How would you describe the character she has created?
3 Where would you most likely meet such a character?
4 How do you think she would answer these questions:
   a) Are you happy with your life?

   b) Do you have any ambitions?
   c) When did you first start living rough?
5 What other questions would you like to ask the character?
6 Now put this character in the hot seat and see what she says when you ask her your questions.

Where do you come from?

What are they saying?

Look at the words and the pictures. Then work out the answers to these questions:

1 What does each of the questions mean?
2 What does each of the answers mean?
3 How do you think the questions and answers were spoken?
4 Where do you think the speakers come from?

What do you call people?

These are all words used in different areas when people are speaking in a friendly way.

1 How many of them have you heard used in this way?
2 Which, if any, are used in your area?
3 Do you ever use any of them?
4 Are there any other words people in your area use in this way?

Local phrase book

You will probably find it easiest to do this activity if you work with other people. Discuss your answers to the questions and then produce a group phrase book.

1 Are there special words in your area for any of these:

child	look at
playing truant	very surprised
sandwich	too hot (of a person)
packed lunch	wood for the bonfire

2 What other words and expressions are special to your area?

3 Use the ideas you have got to make up a local phrase book for your area.

Some definitions

accent : the way in which people from different places pronounce words and sentences.

dialect : the different form of English used by people from different areas and different groups. Different dialects use different words and slightly different grammar.

standard English : the dialect of English that is used when speaking in formal situations. It is normally used for writing.

Shaggy dog story

Ah's not agin dogs. Ah used tioown yan missen yance. Her neame were Jade, an' she were a reet grand dog. She used ti tak ma fer a walk ivvery day wi'oot fail, rain or shine, whether Ah wanted ti goa oot or not. Ti tell t'truth, tekkin' her oot wor a bit of a drag: she dragged ma throo bushes, hedges, trees, ponds – Ah jist cudn't control her. When Ah were finally allowed ti goa back hoam – usually when she were feeling hungry – t'naybors'd phoned police. They thowt Ah'd bin mugged.

▶ Can you work out what this story is all about ?

1. Try reading it aloud to work out what the words mean.
2. Tell it in your own words.
3. Make up a table like this for all the dialect words in the story:
4. Tell this story, or a story of your own, in your own dialect, or a dialect that you know well.

Story word	Standard English	Our local word
agin	against	
Ah's	I am	
bin		

141

You, the reader

When did you learn to read?

Who is right and why?

When I was 4

When I was 6

You never finish learning to read

Earliest memories

Try to remember *your* very first experiences of reading.

1 Can you remember any particular books you liked when you were very young (before you started Juniors)?
2 What were they?
3 How much can you remember about them?
4 What was good about them?
5 Do you have any especially happy memories about reading in those days?
6 Or any especially unhappy memories?
7 Did learning to write help your reading?
8 Talk about your first experiences of reading with a friend and write down all the things you can remember.

Reading at Junior School

What can you remember about your reading experiences at Junior School?
Talk about them with your partner and write down your memories.

1 Did you enjoy reading more, or less?
2 Did you read different kinds of book as you got older?
3 Did you read comics?
4 Did you read information books?
5 Did you have reading tests?
6 Did you have any favourite books or authors?
7 Did you have any hates or fears to do with reading?

Writing

Write a brief history of your life as a reader up to the age of 11.

What do you read now?

What sort of things do you read nowadays? Make up a chart like this.

Type of reading	At home	Examples	At school	Examples
Fiction books	S	The Wind In The Willows	O	The Demon Headmaster
Non- fiction				
Instructions				
Newspapers				
Comics/Mags				
Others				

Key: **O** = *Often* **S** = *Sometimes* **N** = *Never*

What do you enjoy most?

Make a list of the 'ingredients' in the type of reading you most enjoy.
For example, if your favourite type of reading is fiction (stories), list the things you like to find in a story.

Writing

Write about what you are like as a reader now: your interests, your favourite kind of reading, favourite authors, your strengths and weaknesses, how much you read at home, where and when you like reading, your ambitions as a reader.

Is that a fact?

Many of the things people say and write can be divided into **facts** and **opinions**.

Which of these statements are facts and which are opinions?

1 Lemons are more acid than bananas.
2 Bananas are tastier than lemons.
3 One metre is about 3.28 feet.
4 Old people are wiser than young people.
5 Happiness is the most important thing in life.
6 Light travels faster than sound.

Complications

Which of these statements are **facts** and which are **opinions**?

1 Everyone knows that pop music is more fun than classical music.
2 I believe that Skye is one of the Hebridean islands.
3 Of course New York is not the capital of the USA.
4 It is well known that Maths is harder than English.
5 I think owls' eyes are adapted for seeing in very low light.
6 As far as I can see the saxophone was invented later than the clarinet.
7 The fact is that Spurs are a better team than Arsenal.

What kind of fact?

You can place any factual statement into one of three groups:

a) true   ✓

b) false   ✗

c) you are unable to say whether   ?
   it is true or false

Wonder gadgets?

The sticker on page one of the 'Owner's Manual' reveals all: 'For your own safety *this product is not fitted with a laser ...*' Plugged into your stereo, the lighting effect, which is multi-coloured and does pulsate, is fun in a dark room, especially when there's a lot of bass, and might liven up a party. But it comes with a very annoying gyrating sound as the mirror, activated by the music source, vibrates to reflect the light beam on to a wall or ceiling. This spoils quieter music. An over-expensive toy, of limited use and value.

'Which ?' August 1989

What kind of opinion?

You can place any statement of opinion into one of three groups:

d) you agree with it

e) you disagree with it

f) you don't care one way or the other

Laser effect light show in your own home

All the colour and excitement of a laser effect light show can now be produced in your own living room for a fraction of the previous price. The Laser FX is an electronic marvel and will produce for you a pulsating multi-coloured light show perfectly synchronised with your favourite music. Just connect it to your hi–fi, walkman or electric guitar and it will interpret the sounds into colour, patterns and beams that project up to 30 feet, bouncing off ceilings and walls. You've literally never seen anything like it. It's portable, compact (5" x 12") and comes complete with mains cord and all hi-fi connections. 240 volts AC only.

The Laser FX £149.95 TJ412

'The Innovations Report' Autumn 1989

Which is which ?

How would you describe each of these statements? Write down the number of the statement and the letter of the group above it comes in.

A
1. Ivan Lendl won Wimbledon in 1989.
2. Animals should not be killed for food.
3. Meat contains protein.
4. Canberra is the capital of Australia.
5. Australians are more fun to be with than Canadians.
6. Celtic are the best football team in Scotland.
7. Charles Dickens wrote *The mystery of Edwin Drood*.
8. Roald Dahl wrote *Charlie and the chocolate factory*.

B
1. How much of the *Which* article is fact and how much of it is opinion?
2. How many statements of opinion can you find in it?
3. How many statements of fact can you find in it?

Finding it

A library is organised so that you can find your way around it. If you understand how the books are arranged you will find it much easier when you are looking for books.

In the library

Looking for a book ?
Is it fiction or non-fiction ?

Fiction
Books that tell a story which has been made up by the writer.
Novels
Collections of short stories

Non-fiction
Everything else.
These will mainly be information books.

Alphabetical
Fiction is usually arranged in alphabetical order of the authors' surnames.

Subject by subject
Non-fiction books are grouped together by subject. So all the books about fishing are in one place, all those about Chinese cooking in another, and so on.

Reference
In this section you will find the books that you are not usually allowed to take out of the library.
They tend to be the kind of book you dip into when you need a particular fact.
Dictionaries and encyclopedias are usually to be found in this section.

Dewey classification
Most libraries use this sytem. Each subject is given a number. When you look a book up in the catalogue it tells you the number. Then you go to that part of the library to find your book.
000-099 General works
    encyclopedias, school magazines, reading, libraries, newspapers and museums
100-199 Philosophy
    time, logic, individual behaviour, origins of the universe, telepathy, astrology
200-299 Religion
    Christianity, the Bible, prayer, church, Islam, Buddhism, Hinduism, Judaism
300-399 Social sciences
    population, community life, slavery, international relations, economics, law, government, the welfare state, education, transport, customs

400-499 Language
    dictionaries, different languages, grammar, alphabets
500-599 Sciences
    mathematics, astronomy, physics, chemistry, biology, geology, weather, prehistoric life
600-699 Technology
    medicine, health care, engineering, agriculture, gardening, food, clothing, industry, child care
700-799 The arts
    architecture, drawing, painting, music, cinema, theatre, hobbies, sport
800-899 Literature
    great novels, plays and poems in English and other languages, books about novels, plays and poems
900-999 History, geography, biography
    atlases, maps, books on the earth, travel, people's lives, the histories of individual countries

In the book

Alphabetical order

The way round books such as encyclopedias and dictionaries.

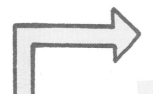

inestimable	152	information

existing state of rest or motion unless acted on by external force.

inestimable (in-**est**-im-ă-bŭl) *adj.* too good, too great, etc., to be estimated; invaluable.

inevitable (in-**ev**-it-ă-bŭl) *adj.* unavoidable; bound to happen or appear. **inevitability** *n.*

inexact *adj.* not exact.

inexhaustible *adj.* that cannot be exhausted. **inexhaustibility** *n.*

inexorable (in-**eks**-er-ă-bŭl) *adj.* relentless.

inexpedient *adj.* not expedient.

inexpensive *adj.* not expensive, cheap.

inexperience *n.* lack of experience. **inexperienced** *adj.*

inexpert *adj.* unskilful.

filtration *n.* (esp.) gradual penetration by small groups, etc. **infiltrator** *n.*

infinite (in-**fin**-it) *adj.* having no limit or end; exceedingly great, vast. **infinitely** *adj.*

infinitesimal (in-fin-i-**tess**-im-ăl) *adj.* extremely small.

infinitive (in-**fin**-i-tiv) *adj. & n.* (verb-form) expressing verbal notion in general way, without subject.

infinitude *n.* infinity.

infinity (in-**fin**-i-ti) *n.* quality of being infinite; boundless number or extent.

infirm *adj.* physically weak; irresolute. **infirmity**

Contents

A general guide at the beginning of a book to tell you what is in it.

Index

A more detailed list of what is in a book. It is arranged in alphabetical order. Sometimes the main pages where a subject is dealt with are printed in bold type.

Nonsense!

Jabberwocky

'Twas brillig, and the slithy toves
Did gyre and gimble in the wabe;
All mimsy were the borogoves,
And the mome raths outgrabe.

'Beware the Jabberwock, my son!
The jaws that bite, the claws that catch!
Beware the Jubjub bird, and shun
The frumious Bandersnatch!'

He took his vorpal sword in hand:
Longtime the manxome foe he sought -
So rested he by the Tumtum tree,
And stood awhile in thought.

And as in uffish thought he stood,
The Jabberwock, with eyes of flame,
Came whiffling through the tulgey wood,
And burbled as it came!

One, two! One, two! And through and through
The vorpal blade went snicker-snack!
He left it dead, and with its head
He went galumphing back.

'And hast thou slain the Jabberwock?
Come to my arms, my beamish boy!
O frabjous day! Callooh! Callay!'
He chortled in his joy.

Twas brillig and the slithy toves
Did gyre and gimble in the wabe;
All mimsy were the borogoves,
And the mome raths outgrabe.

What's it all about?

This poem uses lots of words that sound as if they ought to be proper words but are not. From the sound of them and from the way they are used, you have probably got quite a good idea of what you think they mean. The interesting thing is that different people come up with very different ideas.

1 Write down all the nonsense words in the poem. Against each one write down what you think it means.

Word	Meaning
brillig	evening
slithy	

2 When you have finished compare your definitions with those that other people have written.

3 Choose at least five of the words and use them in your own sentences. (Or even better, try to fit them into a very short story.)

> The attacker was brandishing a vorpal knife. He didn't like the toves because they had long noses.

What do you think?

These sentences all contain one or more of the words from the poem. Do you think they are being used 'correctly'? What are your reasons?

1 While I was digging in the sand I found a strange gimble.
2 Carl and Jayne are both beamish, but Mike is the beamishest person I know.
3 My parents often frumious the dog on Sundays.
4 I had a terrible dream – I was being chased round the Tower of London by a gyre frabjous.
5 Seventeen whiffling Jabberwocks burbled at the vorpal dagger brandished under the Tumtum tree by our brave hero.

You are working for a travel firm selling exotic holidays. Your new line this year is holidays in Wonderland with an opportunity to see strange places and exotic animals and birds.

Jabberwocky is a poem that was made up in Wonderland and it describes some of the wonderful creatures to be seen there.

1 Make up some more creatures and places that can be visited in Wonderland.
2 Write the description of Wonderland to go in the brochure.
3 Write a conversation between you and someone who is thinking of having a Wonderland holiday.

Quindly Quot

Quindly Quot used to tell the story of the Spiggies, their persecution by the Jingoes and how they got their revenge. The trouble is that someone has torn up the only copy of the poem that there is.

4 Some Jingoes are already mad
And some show signs of stress
But most sit by their TVs
Doing less and less.

6 The Spiggy is a strangesome thing,
All quindly quot but fatter.
The Jingoes cut the stems in two
And serve them fried in batter.

5 The Spiggy doesn't like this
Anymore than any plant.
It dreams of Jingoes cut in bits
and sulks because it can't.

1 The Jingoes gave them chemicals
In bags marked 'fertiliser',
Which Spiggies have converted to
A brain cell pulverizer.

2 But down amongst the Gluntike flats
The Spiggies are mutating
And no-one sees the differences
The Spiggies are creating.

7 The doctors blame a virus
Blown in from outer space,
Not dreaming of the Spiggies' plan
To change the Jingo race.

3 The Jingoes grow more lifeless
And grindly grut and fatter
The Spiggies know that one day soon
They'll serve them fried in batter.

8 The Spiggy lives on quietly
Poisoning the nation
Whilst scientists find everything
Except an explanation.

Not the first verse

It would be easier to work out the story of the Jingoes if we knew what the beginning was. Many of the pieces cannot be the beginning because they suggest that something has already happened.

1 Which pieces are these?
2 What clues in each one make you believe that they cannot be the beginning?

Sorting out the story

Now you can begin to work out the right order.

1 What could be the first verse?
2 What could be the last verse?
3 What order do you think makes the best sense ? Write down the numbers in the order. (You may need to try more than one order before you find one that satisfies you.)

In the encyclopedia

Here are some samples of entries in an encyclopedia. You have been asked to prepare short entries about the Jingo and the Spiggy.

Use the information in the poem and add ideas of your own. If you like you can add pictures to illustrate what you write.

A **ANT**
Ants are called social insects because they live in large colonies. There may be as many as a million ants in one nest.

There are three kinds of ant in a colony – a queen, workers and males. The queen mates with a winged male and spends her whole life laying eggs. The female workers cannot lay eggs. They look after the nest, collect food and care for the young. The males do no work beyond mating with the queen.

There are ants in all parts of the world but the coldest. Some have interesting habits. The umbrella ants chew up leaves and use them for growing food. Legionary or Army ants march in vast columns and eat any living thing in their path.

ANTARCTIC
The Antarctic continent is covered with a sheet of ice, thousands of metres thick. Its long coastline is a wall of capes and cliffs. There are mountains and volcanoes. The South Pole is near the centre of a high, windswept plain.

The Antarctic is colder than the Arctic. Even in summer, the temperature rarely rises above freezing point. Algae, mosses and lichens are the only plants. There are no land animals, apart from some tiny insects. But the sea is rich in plankton, fish, seals and whales, and there are penguins and other birds.

ANTEATER
The anteater lives in Central and South America. It breaks open the nests of ants and termites with its powerful claws. Then it

The attack

In the end, the long-planned attack by the Spiggies begins. The first main targets are the central government buildings and the radio station. Write an account of what happens:

1 As a newspaper report.
2 As if you were one of the Spiggies.

Spiggy attack begins

Early today the Spiggy attack on Jingo Land began. At about 3 in the morning a force of Spiggy paratroopers forced its way into the centre of Jingoville and took control of

Using a dictionary

A dictionary provides different kinds of information about a word.

Meaning

Many words have more than one meaning or use.

1 If a word has two completely different meanings or uses, then they are printed separately and numbered.

2 If a word has a number of meanings which are a little different, then they are printed one after another and numbered.

Part of speech

n. (or sub.) = noun
a. (or adj.) = adjective
v. (or vb.) = verb
adv. = adverb

Phrases

Sometimes the dictionary gives a phrase showing how the word is used.

Usage

How the spelling of the word changes when we use it in a sentence.

Compounds

How the word can be changed into other words.

Pronunciation

How the letters of the word are sounded. Which part of the word should be emphasised.

---

frequent

thing. **3.** the number of cycles per second of a carrier wave, a band or group of similar frequencies.
frequent¹ (**free**-kwĕnt) *adj.* happening or appearing often. **frequently** *adv.*
frequent² (fri-**kwent**) *v.* to go frequently to, to be often in (a place).
frequentative (fri-**kwent**-ă-tiv) *adj.* (of a verb) expressing frequent repetition or intensity of an action (e.g. *chatter*).
fresco (**fress**-koh) *n.* (*pl.* frescos) a picture painted on a wall or ceiling before the plaster is dry.
fresh *adj.* **1.** newly made or produced or gathered etc., not stale. **2.** newly arrived. **3.** new or different, not previously known or used. **4.** (of food) not preserved by salting or pickling or tinning or freezing etc. **5.** not salty, not bitter. **6.** (of air or weather) cool, refreshing, (of wind) moderately strong. **7.** bright and pure in colour, not dull or faded. **8.** not weary, feeling vigorous. **9.** (*Amer.*) presumptuous, forward. —**freshly** *adv.*, **freshness** *n.*
freshen *v.* to make or become fresh.
freshwater *adj.* of fresh (not salty) water, not of the sea. *freshwater fish.*
Fresnel lens (frĕ-**nel**) a kind of lens composed of ring-shaped sections of differing curvature, so that a short focal length can be achieved with a thin lens.
fret¹ *v.* (**fretted**, fretting) **1.** to make or become unhappy, to worry, to vex. **2.** to wear away by gnawing or rubbing. —*n.* a state of unhappiness or worry, vexation.
fret² *n.* a bar or ridge on the finger-board of a guitar etc., as a guide for the fingers to press the strings at the correct place.
fretful *adj.* constantly worrying or crying. **fretfully** *adv.*
fretsaw *n.* a very narrow saw fixed in a frame, used for cutting thin wood in ornamental patterns.
fretted *adj.* (of a ceiling etc.) decorated with carved or embossed work.
fretwork *n.* carved work in decorative patterns, especially in wood cut with a fretsaw.
Freudian (**froi**-di-ăn) *adj.* of Sigmund Freud, an Austrian physician (1856–1939), the founder of psychoanalysis, or his theories.
friable (**fry**-ă-bŭl) *adj.* easily crumbled.
friar *n.* a man who is a member of certain Roman Catholic religious orders (especially the Franciscans, Augustinians, Dominicans, and Carmelites), working among people in the outside world and not as enclosed orders. **friar's balsam,** a kind of oil used as an inhalant.
friary *n.* a monastery of friars.

fricassee (frik-ă-s...
fried pieces of mea...
friction *n.* **1.** the ...
against another. **2.** ...
surface to anothe...
3. conflict between ...
ideas or personaliti...
Friday *n.* the day ...
Thursday.
fridge *n.* (*informal*) ...
fried *see* fry¹.
friend *n.* **1.** a person ...
terms of mutual af...
of sexual or family l...
or quality, *darkness* ...
helper or sympathize...
ber of the Society of ...
friendship *n.*
friendless *adj.* withou...
friendly *adj.* (friendlier ...
friend, kindly. **2.** (of ...
helpful. **friendliness** ...
match, a match play ...
and not in competiti...
Friendly Society, a ...
mutual benefit of its m...
illness or old age.
Friesian (**free**-zhăn) *n.* ...
large black-and-white ...
nally from Friesland, a...
Netherlands.
frieze *n.* a band of sculpt...
round the top of a wall o...
frigate (**frig**-ăt) *n.* a small ...
vessel or a small destroye...
fright *n.* **1.** sudden great ...
lous-looking person or th...
frighten *v.* **1.** to cause frig...
fright, *he doesn't frighten e...*
or compel by fright, *frigh...*
concealing it. □ **be fright...**
afraid of.
frightful *adj.* **1.** causing f...
3. (*informal*) very great, ...
tremely bad. **frightfully** *adv...*
frigid (**frij**-id) *adj.* **1.** intensel...
cold and formal in manner.
frigidity (fri-**jid**-i-ti) *n.*
frill *n.* **1.** a gathered or ple...
trimming attached at one ed...
necessary extra, *simple ac...*
with no frills. **frilled** *adj.*, **frill...**
fringe *n.* **1.** an ornamental edg...
ing threads or cords etc. **2.** s...
sembling this. **3.** front hair c...
hang over the forehead. **4.** the ...
area or a group etc. —**fringe** ...
orate with a fringe. **2.** to form ...
□ **fringe benefits,** benefits ...
provided for an employee in a...
wages or salary.

152

1 Using the dictionary page headed **frequent**, what does the word *fresh* mean in each of these sentences?

  a He was a fanatic for fresh air.
  b She had a fresh complexion.
  c He is fresh from his world tour.
  d This is a fresh idea.
  e She only fishes in fresh water.
  f He has dropped a dozen fresh eggs.
  g The room was filled with fresh flowers.
  h 'Don't be so fresh!'
  i She decided to make a fresh start.
  j He always insisted on fresh fish.

2 Write down the words from the same dictionary page which are missing in these sentences.

  a It was a _____ occurrence for him to be away from school.
  b Keep away from the edge of the cliff because it is _____.
  c There are the ruins of the _____, the oldest religious building in the county.
  d This bread is _____ baked.
  e He was so worried when I saw him; he was in a real _____.

Write your own definitions

Real words

Write your own dictionary definition for each of the words in the list below. Try to give all the information that the definitions on page 152 give.

school	scold
scoop	scoff
score	

Crazy definitions

polygon (polly-gone) *n.* a dead parrot

bulrush (bull-rush) *n.* a cattle stampede

Write your own crazy definitions for these words (or choose different words of your own and write crazy definitions for them).

dragonfly	succeed
lugger	syntax
paradise	usher
scullery	

Jabberwocky

If you have read the poem *Jabberwocky* (on page 148), you will probably have some ideas about the meanings of these words. Choose five and write a full dictionary definition of each one:

bandersnatch	jubjub
beamish	manxome
borogove	mimsy
brillig	mome
frabjous	outgrabe
frumious	rath
galumph	slithy
gimble	toves
gyre	tulgey
jabberwock	tumtum

People, places, and words

What do you think:
1 The mother feels like?
2 The mother is saying?
3 The child feels?
4 The child is likely to say in reply?
How do you think the words will be spoken?
Write the conversation that takes place.

More situations

How did she say it?

1 Look at each of the four pictures on the facing page. Decide what is happening.
2 Think about what the girl might be saying.
3 Think about how she might be saying it.
4 Look at the list of words below. Choose the best word to describe her tone of voicein each picture.

agreeable	free-and-easy	polite
amiable	friendly	relaxed
annoyed	frightened	resentful
casual	indignant	respectful
chatty	irritated	warm
crawling	mild	
cross	offended	

The conversation

Choose one of the pictures and write the whole conversation. Write not only what is said, but also how it is said. Write it as script:

Girl: *(nervously)* I'm very pleased to meet you, ma'am.
Mayoress: *(warmly)* It's good to see you after all I've heard. Tell me...

— Role play

Situation one

A is the 11-year-old son or daughter.
B is the mother or father.
A normally has to be in by 6.30 in the evenings during winter, unless s/he is with an adult.

Role A instructions

You have been invited by some friends to go and see a film. Unfortunately it ends at 7.10, which means that you would not get home until 7.30. You very much want to see the film with your friends and this is the only time when you can all go together.

Role B instructions

You think it is sensible to insist that **A** gets home by 6.30 on winter's evenings – whatever other people's children may do. You do not see why you should change this rule just so that **A** can see a film. **A** can go to the Saturday afternoon showing.

Situation two

A and **B** are brothers or sisters or brother and sister. **A** is 12 and **B** is 10. It is a weekday evening and the family have just finished having tea. **A** is clearing up the dishes and **B** is playing with model cars.

Role A instructions

You always have to clear up after tea – and just because you are the oldest. **B** doesn't have homework and you seem to get more and more – so why should you have to do housework as well? And there's a programme on TV you want to watch this evening...and you've got an extra lot of homework to do...

Role B instructions

A is older than you and gets all sorts of things you don't – more pocket-money, staying up later, more grown-up treatment ... So it's fair that **A** should have to do more jobs around the place.

Note If you aren't sure about how to tackle a role play, look on page 135.

What line of business are you in?

There was a computer salesperson, and a sports commentator, and a doctor, and a TV cook, and an antiques expert, and a garage mechanic, and a disc jockey, and a plumber, and a...

When people speak, they often use a different type of language for different occasions. At work, some people might use words which apply only to their job, and which they would not use in normal conversation at home.

Look at the sentences below.

1 Who said what?
2 How do you know?

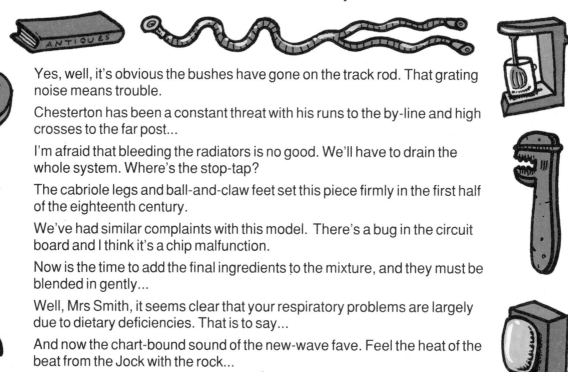

Yes, well, it's obvious the bushes have gone on the track rod. That grating noise means trouble.

Chesterton has been a constant threat with his runs to the by-line and high crosses to the far post...

I'm afraid that bleeding the radiators is no good. We'll have to drain the whole system. Where's the stop-tap?

The cabriole legs and ball-and-claw feet set this piece firmly in the first half of the eighteenth century.

We've had similar complaints with this model. There's a bug in the circuit board and I think it's a chip malfunction.

Now is the time to add the final ingredients to the mixture, and they must be blended in gently...

Well, Mrs Smith, it seems clear that your respiratory problems are largely due to dietary deficiencies. That is to say...

And now the chart-bound sound of the new-wave fave. Feel the heat of the beat from the Jock with the rock...

Technical terms

Many different activities require special words: they have their own technical terms.

1 Think about the subjects you are studying at school. Make a list of technical terms that you use in school.
2 Think about any special interest you may have (bikes? pop? underwater basket weaving?) What technical terms does it have?

3 Choose one of the topics you have thought of. Make a list of all the technical terms that you can remember. For each one write a short definition explaining it to someone who has no special knowledge of that subject.

Getting the facts straight

Here are the opening sentences of extracts from three pieces of factual writing. What do you think each book is about? What makes you think this?

a) Once upon a time there was a teeny-tiny little waif who lived on an island a squillion miles from anywhere!

b) The radio presenter's job may look very easy – he sits in a studio, chats into a microphone, and puts on a record.

c) The secret of consistently good wheelies is to know your balance point.

These sentences come from the three extracts and follow on from the opening sentences you have already read. They have been jumbled up.

1 Work out which sentences come from which books.
2 Work out the correct order for the sentences in each book.

a How did it happen?
b While a record is playing, the presenter picks out the next one, puts it onto a second turntable, and sets the needle in exactly the right place.
c Then lean back, don't jerk, until you reach the balance point.
d That's the name of a hospital in Melbourne.
e For a start there is the studio and its equipment to learn about.
f Then, one day, she appeared in a wibbly soap and released some stonkin' teen-anthem toons and became the gigantic-est pipsqueak popstrel on the planet.
g This is called 'cueing up' a record, and means that the music will start as soon as he switches the turntable on.
h One way is to get a friend to help by lifting the front wheel (with you on the bike of course) until you find the point where you feel comfortable.
i To start, put your leading foot on the pedal set at about two o'clock.
j She was born in Bethlehem!
k Once you're balanced, keep pedalling at all times.

You, the writer

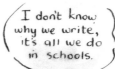

Discussion

Talk about these questions. At the end of your discussion you are going to tell the rest of the class what your group thinks. This reporting back should last about five minutes.

1 You have to do a lot of writing in school. What is it all for?
2 Do you like writing? What are your reasons?
3 Do you write in different ways for different people? If so, why is this?
4 What makes a good piece of writing?
5 How different would life be in school if nobody knew how to write?
6 How different would life for everybody be outside school if nobody knew how to write?
7 How important is it to you to be able to write?
8 Are there any other important things you would like to say about writing?

Writing

Choose one of these topics to write about. Think about the discussion you have had in your group and in the class. Use some of the ideas that have come up and add new ideas of your own.

1 Many people think that writing is the most important aspect of work at school. What are their reasons? Do you think they are right? What are your reasons?

2 What is your earliest (or most vivid) memory of writing something? Describe your memory and explain what you think was special about that particular piece of writing.

3 Think about the different ways in which you have used writing in the past and the way that you use it now (both in and out of school). Think about your own feelings about writing. Now write about 'Me as writer'.

Group work

1 In your group take it in turns to read out what you have written.

2 When each person has finished reading, make comments to help them improve what they have written:

a) Does it all make good sense?

b) Is it in the best order?

c) Are there ways in which it could be made stronger?

d) Are there any other improvements that could be made?

159

*W*riting: the mechanics' guide

Making a piece of writing is a bit like building a car...

Purpose

A car can't go anywhere without an engine: it's dead. Writing needs an engine, too; we call it the purpose. Writing which has no purpose is often lifeless and doesn't seem to be going anywhere.

The purpose might be:
- to give information
- to persuade someone to do something
- to help you to remember.
... there are lots of different purposes for writing.

Before you start writing you should ask yourself: 'What is the purpose of this piece of writing?' If you can answer that question then your writing has an engine, something that will give it drive.

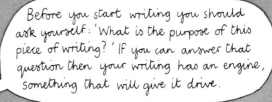

Audience

It's all very well having an engine, but you need to guide the car so you need a steering wheel. Writing needs to travel in certain directions too; it needs an audience to guide it.

Before you start writing you should ask yourself: 'Who is this writing for?'

It may be for:
- you (notes, diaries, jottings etc)
- a teacher
- friends
- other people in the class
- someone you've never met
... there are lots of different audiences for writing.

Form

All cars have a shape; the shape of a mini is different from that of a Rolls Royce. Writing needs a shape, too; a form which holds all the parts together.

Before you start writing you should be clear about the form of your writing. Is it:
- a list?
- notes?
- a play?
- a poem?
- an essay?
- or something else?
... what form will it take?

Writing	Purpose	Audience	Form
Life in a medieval village	Describing what life was like then	Teacher	Diary of one day

Making a list

1 On your own, look though all your school work (not just English) written in the last two weeks.

2 Make a list of all the
- purposes
- audiences
- forms
you have tackled.

3 If you have written other pieces outside school work (perhaps letters to a friend, notes to the milkman, shopping lists) write these down as well.

4 Share your list with the group. (They may have thought of things you had forgotten.)

5 Together make a group list like the one on the left.

6 Design a poster to show the rest of the class the range of writing your group has tackled. Make your poster as lively and attractive as possible. Think about:
- the purpose of the poster
- the audience of the poster
- the best form (shape and design) for the poster

7 Look at the posters other groups have made. Compare them with yours. What are the good and bad features of each one?

161

Sounds and letters

In English we use patterns of letters to write down the spoken words of the language. We can even use letters to write down sounds which are not strictly words.

How would you write each of these sounds below ? Write down the sound each one makes, without using dictionary words. Use the sounds of letters to make up new sound words.

Experiment

When you learned to read, you learned to associate certain letters with certain sounds. You can use these patterns to help you read words you have never seen or heard before. Try saying the words in these three lists.

A	B	C
dit	pough	ngsi
rotched	anglet	thpa
thrupping	tanchor	shbu
chooble	gep	oneph
dight	rislant	tplo

1 Which words were you unsure about?
2 Were there any words that you thought could have been said in two different ways?
3 Which list was the easiest to say?
4 Which list was the most difficult?
5 Why were some words easier and others harder?

Why spelling is complicated

One of the reasons why English spelling is complicated is because there are nearly twice as many sounds as letters.

Consonants

There are 23 consonant sounds in English. In this list they are shown by the letters printed darker than the others:

bat	**k**it	**p**et	**th**is
chop	**l**ip	**r**at	**t**op
did	**m**at	**s**at	**v**est
foot	mea**s**ure	**sh**oppi**ng**	**w**ith
get	**n**ot	**th**in	**y**et
hat			**z**ip

There are 21 consonant letters:

b c d f g h j k l m n p q r s t v w x y z

For each of the consonant sounds in the first list, find one or two other words that contain the sound: one that spells it as it is spelled in the list and if possible one that spells it in a different way. For example, for the **k** sound, you might write:

    kind   account

Underline the letters that spell the sound.

Vowels

Vowels are more complicated. There are 20 vowel sounds, but only 5 vowel letters. This means that the letters have to work very hard and do more than one job.

1 Say each of these words and work out what the letter 'e' is doing in each one:

hearth	break	berth
mend	there	pretty
see	height	fear

2 Say each of these words and then write down how the vowel sound in each one is spelled:

mine	by	fight
height	die	dye
aisle		

3 See how many spellings you can find for each of these vowel sounds:

    or as in sort
    ay as in day
    oo as in moon

Sound words

English has a number of words that make the sound they describe:

1 See how many more you can think of. Make a list of them.
2 Choose three of your words and think of interesting and unusual ways of writing them (as we have done in the illustration).
3 Choose one of the pictures on the opposite page. Write about the picture using as many good sound words as you can.

163

*I*t's different... *when you write it*

Thinking

What's going on in this picture ?
What are they doing ?
Why do you think they are doing this ?
Where is it happening ?

Think about these points and then make up a story that explains what is going on in the picture.

Telling

Now share your ideas with a partner.

1 Decide who will tell their story first.
2 Tell your own story as vividly as you can.
3 Listen carefully to your partner's story.
4 Can you think of any other stories that might explain the picture ? If so, tell them, too.

Writing

1 Choose one of the stories you told your partner.
2 Remember all the details that you can - and add any extra ones you can think of now.
3 Write your story for your partner to read.

Reading

Work with the same partner as before.

1 Swap stories.
2 As you read your partner's story compare it with what you heard when the story was told aloud. What differences do you notice between the two versions ?
3 Make a list of any differences you have noticed.
4 Discuss with your partner how the two stories have changed between telling them and writing them down. Why do you think they have changed ?

Another discussion

Clare, Ross and Zoe talked about this picture. First of all they took it in turns to make up a story about the picture. This is the beginning of the story Ross told. –is a pause, and / is where the meaning changes.

Once upon a time there was a girl called Sally / one day her mum ran out of food so she went shopping in Gateway/they walked up to the shops / her mum had to push the baby cos they had a baby / when they were walking down the street past Kiosk and then past the sweetshop Sally saw a boy lying down on the pavement on top of a towel / the boy was eating fire / she went over to him and asked why are you doing that – and he said well you see my father hasn't got much money so he makes me come out here on the streets to earn some – he said I have a very special – wisdom though if you stand on top of me when I eat fire you can make any wish and itll come true / go on you can do it now / so Sally got on top of the boy very carefully so she wouldnt hurt him and made a wish / she wished she could become an egyptian princess for the day / suddenly smoke started to swirl round her green smoke purple smoke red smoke / she suddenly appeared in this palace a big palace with lots of servants areound her / she was in a most gorgeous robe in gold sequins and silver / she had a long dangling necklace with red rubies on them

1　Look at the picture they were talking about.
2　Read Ross's spoken story and his written story.
3　Compare the two and make a list of the most important differences between them:
　　● in the way he tackled telling the story
　　● in the kinds of sentence he used
　　● in the words he used.
4　Why do you think there were these differences between the two ?

Then they talked about this picture and made up more stories. When they had finished discussing it they wrote their stories down. This is the beginning of Ross's written story. It has been printed as he wrote it.

A Step in Time

'Mum! Mum!' I yelled 'Mum where are you?'
'Down here' called my mum from the kitchen.
'Well you know Claire's party tomorrow'I began
'Yes dear' replied my mum
'Well I've got nothing to wear!' I complained.
'Why don't you wear your pretty dress,'suggested my mum.
'Mum you don't get it' I said 'Its a fancy-dress party!'
'Oh' exclaimed my mum 'I'll have to take you shopping then'
So mum drove us into town to pick something for me to wear. As we were walking along the crowded street I noticed a boy lying down on the pavement. He had no top on and looked quite dirty. He appeared to be eating fire. He beconed me over to him so I went to see what he wanted. He whispered to me 'I have a special wisdom that is when someone stands on me and I eat fire they can make a wish and it will come true.' He pointed to his stomach. 'Here you try' he asked. I cautiously steped on to him not to hurt him. He began to swallow a stick of fire. I made a wish I wish I could have the perfect fancy-dress costume. Suddenly green smoke swirled around me. Then red smoke, purple smoke, blue smoke, white smoke. I suddenly appeared in someones dressing-room. I looked down at myself and had a surprise. I was in a most colourful clowns out-fit. It had got sequins and silver buttons. It was perfect.

Storyboard

How it all started...

How it ended...

Look at the pictures on the opposite page.

1 Think of a story

Think of a story, or more than one if you can.
What is happening at the beginning – who is the
person in the pictures? What has happened by the
time we reach the last two pictures?
Make sure that your story links the beginning
and the end so that they both make sense.

2 Tell your partner

Tell your partner all the stories you have
thought of. Listen to your partner's stories.
Talk about them.

3 Write the beginning

Make up the first two or three sentences of the
story.

4 Write some more beginnings

Think of other ways your story (or a
different story) could begin. Write these
beginnings, too.

5 Swap with your partner

Read your partner's beginnings. Let your
partner read yours.

6 Think about it

Think about your partner's beginnings. Decide
which one(s) you like and why.

7 Discuss it

Tell your partner what you think. Listen to
what your partner thinks. See if you can add
any more ideas to each other's work. Make
suggestions about how each of you might
improve your beginning sentences.

8 Start writing

Decide which beginning you are going to use
and write the rest of the story.

Poems for two voices

You will need a partner to work with. You are going to write some poems which the two of you can practise reading aloud.

The idea in all these poems is that two people speak alternate lines. They are dialogue poems ('dialogue' is another word for conversation or speech).

The 'answering-back' poem

The first speaker is telling off the second speaker. It might be an older sister telling off a younger brother, or a team captain telling off someone in the team. The second speaker 'thinks' the words he or she would like to say in reply:

I thought I told you to tidy your room.
All right... give me a chance... don't nag.
I thought I told you to clean your shoes.
All right... give me a chance... don't nag.
I thought I told you to do your work.
All right... give me a chance... don't nag.
I thought I told you, don't answer back!
I thought I told you, don't nag!

1 Decide what the situation in your poem is going to be. Who is doing the telling off or giving the orders?
2 Make a list of things the first speaker can say. Make a long list and then choose the ones you like best. Arrange them in the most effective order.
3 Work out what the second speaker is going to say. It might be a different way of answering back each time or it might be the same words each time.
4 Think of a good way of ending the poem.
5 Practise reading the poem together. Make any changes which will make it sound better.
6 Write your final version of the poem.
7 Practise reading it again until you are ready to give a performance of it.

The 'secret thoughts' poem

There is only one person in this, but the first speaker says what the person actually says and the second speaker says what the person is secretly thinking.

> George! How lovely to see you!
> *Oh no, not him again!*
> We haven't seen you for ages.
> *How can I get rid of him?*
> You must come in and have some tea.
> *Of course he will, he always does.*
> You're looking very fit and well.
> *Just as sick and scruffy as ever.....*

1 Think of a situation where what you might be thinking is very different from what you actually say.
2 Work on the poem with your partner in the same way as for the 'answering-back' poem.

The 'cross-purposes' poem

Sometimes people appear to be having a conversation when really they are not listening to each other properly, and may not be talking about the same thing:

> **Teatime**.
> Henry, would you like a boiled egg?
> *Mum, I've hurt my finger.*
> Just pop it in the saucepan when the water's boiled.
> *It could be infected.*
> Should be lovely. Free-range, fresh today.
> *It's been bleeding for ages.*
> Only four minutes, you like it runny.
> *I'll need some disinfectant.*
> And not too much salt, remember.
> *I'd better put a plaster on it.*
> Can you slice the top off by yourself?
> *I did it playing soldiers...*
> Well, you know where the bread-knife is.
> *...At the bottom of the garden.*
> And mind you don't cut your fingers.
> *Mum, what's for tea?*

Try your hand at writing (and performing) a 'cross-purposes' poem.

169

What did it look like?

Can you describe one of the coats below so that someone looking at the pictures would know which one you had chosen?

1 On your own choose one of the coats.
2 Do not write down its letter.
3 Write a detailed description of it, so that someone can work out which one you have chosen. No cheating! You can only describe the coat. You must not give clues, such as where it is on the page.
4 In pairs swap books.
5 Read your partner's description.

6 Try to work out which coat your partner has described.
7 Talk to your partner:
   ● Did each of you choose the right one?
   ● Was it difficult or easy?
   ● What made it difficult or easy?
   ● How could your description be improved?

Dream monster

You have a go

How would you describe them?

1 Choose one of the dream monsters.
2 Give it a name that really suits it.
3 Write a detailed description of it so that someone who had not seen the picture would be able to imagine what it looked like.

Tips

When you are writing your description, try to include your ideas about these points:

- what colour(s) it is
- what its skin looks (and feels) like
- how big you think it is
- its shape
- what its head is like (or heads, if it has more than one)
- how it moves
- the sort of noise you think it makes

It's easy when...

These pictures come from a book about hairdressing. They show how to make a French plait. Unfortunately the explanations that go with each picture are missing. See if you can work out what they ought to say.

1 Look at the pictures carefully. Work out exactly what is happening in each one.
2 For each picture, make rough notes describing what is being done.
3 Now turn these notes into a simple and clear explanation of what to do. Imagine that you are writing for someone of your own age, who knows nothing at all about the subject.

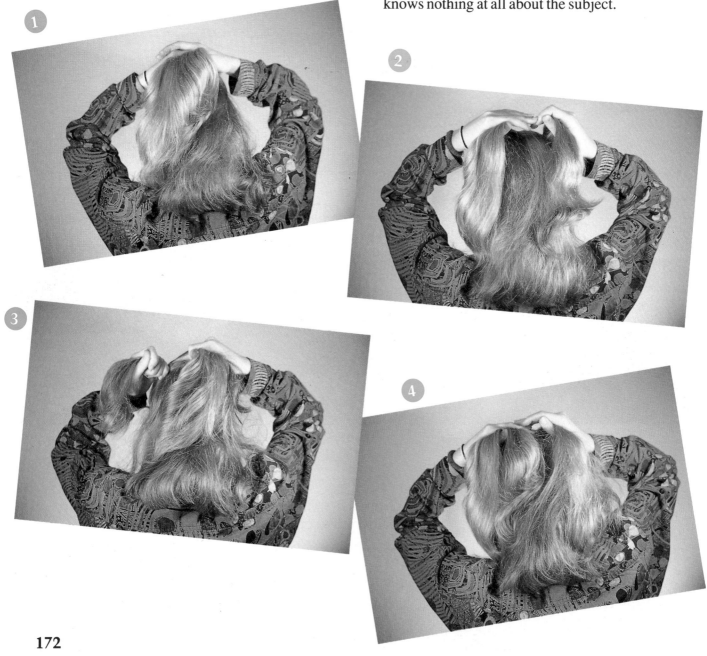

...you know how

School - the unofficial guide

When you started at your new school, you may have been given a *Guide for new pupils*. Have you ever thought that the wrong people write these guides? Would they be better written by other students? This is your chance to produce your own unofficial guide: a *First day survival kit* for new students.

Research

Begin by collecting information and ideas. For example:

- questions you need to answer
- essential information to include
- advice you wish people had given you

It can come from:

- your own memories of early days at the school
- talking to other people at school

Make notes as you go along, otherwise, you will forget things.

Sorting it out

Now sort your notes. Divide them into three groups:

1 What I must include
2 What I would like to include
3 What I will put in if I am short of ideas

Decide on the order that you want things to go in.

> SCHOOL
> METLEY / GUIDE ← boring title
> ?
> (Hallo!) If you are
> ~~you're~~ reading this on
> your first day, you are probably
> wondering what the next [five? year(s)
> is going to be like.

First draft

Now write a first draft of your guide.

Drafting

Work with a partner. Read your partner's first draft, while s/he reads yours. Discuss them:

1 What are the good points of each one?
2 Which parts could be left out of each one?
3 Is there anything they both miss out, which should be included?

Now decide how to combine them. Decide:

1 What to take from each draft.
2 What to add.
3 What order to put things in.
4 Who will write which bits.

Final version

Now write your final version.

> A METLEY WELCOME
>
> If you are reading this on your first day at Metley, you are probably wondering what the next year will be like.

*P*unctuation

Capital letters

Capital letters are used for these purposes:

1 As the first letter of a sentence.

> Have a nice day.

2 For the personal pronoun 'I'.

> Last week I went to the zoo.

3 At the beginning of a new piece of direct speech. (See page 181.)

> At last he said,'We won !'

4 For the first letter of proper nouns.

> People's names: Deirdre Blackadder
> Places: Brentwood
> Titles of books, plays, films, TV programmes:
>   Oxford English Programme
> Days of the week: Wednesday
> Months of the year: January
> Planets and stars: Jupiter

5 For the first letter of titles of people and organisations.

> Lady Windermere
> Foreign Minister
> Royal Society for the Protection of Birds

6 For initials in people's names.

> W. Shakespeare

7 For initial letters used in abbreviations.

> JP
> IBA
> NSPCC

Full stops, question marks and exclamation marks

Normal sentences must end with one of these three marks. . ? !

Statements normally end with a **full stop**.

> It is easy when you know how .

A **question** normally ends with a **question mark**.

> Do you understand what I mean ?

Exclamation marks are used to mark an **exclamation**, or a **forceful statement**.

> If only you would listen to what I am saying !

> **Warning!**
> If you use too many
> exclamation marks,
> readers will get
> very tired of them!

Abbreviations

If a word is shortened, or abbreviated, then you usually put a full stop after it.

> **M.K.**Thomas
> 4.5 kilometres **N.**
> **Pa.** (Pennsylvania)
> **Col.** (Colonel)

There are a number of exceptions to this.

1   Abbreviations made up only of capital letters do not need full stops.

> **ANC**   **OUP**   **TUC**

2   Abbreviations that make up words (acronyms) do not need full stops.

> **ASH** (Action on Smoking and Health)
> **COSIRA** (Council for Small Industries in Rural Areas)

3   These abbreviations do not need full stops.

> **Mr Mrs Ms M** (Monsieur) **Mme** (Madame)
> **Mlle** (Mademoiselle) **Dr St Revd**
> **p** (=penny or pence)

Commas

Commas are used to help the reader's eye as it passes over the page of print. If we did not use them at all, sentences could become difficult, or even impossible, to understand. Try reading the paragraph below, which has been printed without commas.

> On my birthday Suzie helped Maria and me set up my new model-car racing-track. First we opened up the box and took out all the pieces: 2 Grand Prix racing cars 1 mains converter 2 racing controllers 15 straight track lengths 1 chicane 6 curved track lengths.
>
> Suzie suggested that we should start off by putting the track together so that is what we did but just as we had got the end curves set up Dad came in to tell us it was time for lunch.
>
> After lunch which was roast chicken and lots of vegetables followed by baked apples and custard we got on with the racing-track again.

As you can see, it would be much easier to read if there were some commas in the right places.

Three uses of commas

1. To separate the items in a list.

> On my birthday Suzie helped Maria and me set up my new model-car racing-track. First we opened up the box and took out all the pieces: 2 Grand Prix racing cars, 1 mains converter, 2 racing controllers, 15 straight track lengths, 1 chicane, 6 curved track lengths.

2. To separate the clauses in a sentence.

> Dad suggested that we should start off by putting the track together, so that is what we did, but just as we had got the end curves set up, Dad came in to tell us it was time for lunch.

3. To mark off phrases that are separate from the main part of the sentence.

> After lunch, which was roast chicken and lots of vegetables followed by baked apples and custard, we got on with the racing-track again.

Apostrophes

Apostrophes are used for two purposes:

1   To show possession (that something belongs to somebody).

2   To show omission (that something has been missed out).

Possession

1   Normally you add **'s**.

> That is the dog**'s** basket, not the cat**'s**.
> That is Maria**'s** book.

2   When the word is a plural ending in **s**, we just add **'**.

> That is the girls' tennis ball.

Notice that these words do not have an apostrophe.

> hers   ours   yours   theirs

When its means 'of it', you should not put an apostrophe.

Omission

When we are writing informally, or writing speech, we often use shortened forms. In these cases, the apostrophe shows where the letters have been missed out.

he is	→	heis	→	he's
they are	→	theyare	→	they're
I do not	→	I donot	→	I don't
it is	→	itis	→	it's

Writing down speech

There are two ways in which you can write down the words that someone says:

 1 script

2 direct speech

Script is normally used for plays. Direct speech is most commonly used in stories.

Script

1 The names of the speakers are put in in capital letters on the left-hand side of the page.

2 The words spoken are written, without any special punctuation, a little way to the right. The speeches should all start at the same point in the line.

3 Information about an individual character who is speaking, is put in the speech. It is put in brackets and underlined.

4 Information about other things that happen, including sounds and actions, is given a line to itself. It is put in brackets and underlined. Characters, names in this information are put in capital letters.

(**TINTIN** opens the door. There is a **MAN** standing there.)

MAN: Mr Tintin?

TINTIN: Yes.

MAN: Mr Tintin. I see from this morning's paper that you are going to try and find Red Rackham's treasure. Is that so?

TINTIN: Yes, it is. But...

MAN: Good. In that case I shall accompany you!...As for the treasure, I shall be satisfied with a half share... Here is my card...

(**MAN** offers him a card. **TINTIN** takes it and looks at it.)

TINTIN: (Amazed) Is...is that really your name?

MAN: So it seems, young man.

TINTIN: Look, Captain...

(He shows the card to **CAPTAIN HADDOCK**.)

CAPTAIN: (Even more amazed than **TINTIN**.) Blistering barnacles!

180

Direct speech

1 Each piece of speech is enclosed between double or single inverted commas. In books single inverted commas are normally used. In school students are often taught to use double inverted commas.

2 Every new piece of speech must begin with a capital letter, even if it is not the first word in the sentence

3 Each piece of speech must end with a full stop or an exclamation mark or a question mark before the concluding inverted commas...

4 ...unless the sentence is going to continue, when it ends with a comma. This also comes before the concluding inverted commas.

5 When a piece of speech comes in the middle of a sentence it must have a comma (or sometimes a colon) just before the opening inverted commas.

6 For each new speaker you start a new line and indent.

7 When something happens, or there is a sound, or you want to describe how someone felt, you just write it as part of the story.

Tintin opened the door to find a strange man standing there.

'Mr Tintin?' asked the man.

'Yes.'

'Mr Tintin,' said the man, 'I see from this morning's paper that you are going to try and find Red Rackham's treasure. Is that so?'

'Yes, it is,' replied Tintin, puzzled. 'But...'

'Good. In that case I shall accompany you!...As for the treasure, I shall be satisfied with a half share... Here is my card.'

The man offered him a card. When Tintin saw what was printed on it he was amazed. He asked,' Is...is that really your name?'

'So it seems, young man.'

Tintin showed the card to Captain Haddock.

'Look, Captain...' he began.

'Blistering barnacles!' exclaimed the Captain.

S pelling

Ways to better spelling

Nearly everybody finds some spellings difficult. Different people have different ways of solving spelling problems.

Write it down and try it out

Spellings are patterns and our brains are good at remembering patterns. If you are not sure which of two or three spellings is right, try writing them all out on a piece of paper — which of them looks right?

Use a dictionary

If you think you know how the word starts, look it up in a dictionary. If you are not sure how it starts, try different versions out on paper first and look them up in the dictionary to find out which one is right.
Check pages 152-153 for using a dictionary.

Look for patterns

English spelling is not chaotic. Three-quarters of all words are spelled according to regular patterns. As you are reading and writing, try to be aware of the patterns of letters used to spell particular sounds.

Look for word families

Words go in families:-

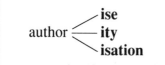

This family consists of four words. In all of them author is spelled the same. **–ity –ise –isation** are spelled in the same way as they are in other words (modernise, modernity, modernisation, for example). If you look out for families like this, you will find spelling gets easier.

Learn the rules for changes

Many words have to be changed according to how they are used in a sentence. We have to add bits onto the end of them:

– s/es	one boss	...	several boss**es**
	I pass	...	she pass**es**
– ed	she taps	...	I tapp**ed**
	he rakes	...	I rak**ed**
– ing	I skated	...	they are skat**ing**
	I tip	...	we are tipp**ing**

If you learn the rules you will avoid a lot of mistakes.

These rules are explained on pages 184–185.

Keep a spelling book

Either get a special notebook, or use the back of an exercise book. Write down the words you find difficult, so that you can look them up easily.

Use words

Never be put off from using a new word just because you are not sure how to spell it.

Read books

Read regularly. Reading will not make everyone a perfect speller, but it is difficult to be a really good speller if you never read anything at all.

Making plurals

Plural means 'more than one'.
Most words follow these rules:

1 Normally, just add **s**.

book	→ book**s**
complication	→ complication**s**

2 Words that end in **–s**, add **es**.

glass	→	glass**es**
genius	→	genius**es**

3 Words that end in **–x** and **–z**, add **es**

box	→	box**es**
buzz	→	buzz**es**

4 Words that end in **–ch** and **–sh**, add **es**.

branch	→	branch**es**
bush	→	bush**es**

5 Words that end in **–f** or **–fe** change the ending to **ve** and add **s**.

calf	→	cal**ves**
wife	→	wi**ves**

Exceptions

beliefs	chiefs	dwarfs	griefs
gulfs	proofs	roofs	

6 Words that end in **–y**. If the letter before the **y** is a vowel, just add **s**.

day	→	day**s**
boy	→	boy**s**

If the letter before the **y** is a consonant, change the **y** to **ies**.

baby	→	bab**ies**
spy	→	sp**ies**

7 Words that end in **–o** : usually just need an **s**.

piano	→	piano**s**.

Exceptions

A few words add **es**.

buffalo**es**	mango**es**
cargo**es**	mosquito**es**
domino**es**	motto**es**
echo**es**	potato**es**
go**es**	tomato**es**
grotto**es**	tornado**es**
halo**es**	torpedo**es**
hero**es**	volcano**es**

8 Words that stay the same in the plural:

aircraft	deer	sheep

9 Words that change in a different way:

child	→	children
man	→	men
foot	→	feet
goose	→	geese
mouse	→	mice
tooth	→	teeth
woman	→	women

10 Some Latin and Greek words change in a different way:

crisis	→	crises
formula	→	formulae

Adding –ing and –ed

When we use verbs we have to change them according to the sentence they are in:
I **walk** to school. I **walked** to school yesterday, and I am **walking** to school now.

1 Normally you just add **ing** and **ed**.

The rules that follow describe the main exceptions.

2 Words with one syllable, with a long vowel, ending in – **e**. Remove the **e** and add **ed** and **ing**.

| rake | rak**ed** | rak**ing** |
| dare | dar**ed** | dar**ing** |

But note :		
age	ag**ed**	age**ing**
queue	queu**ed**	queue**ing**

3 Words with one syllable, with a short vowel, ending in a single consonant. Double the consonant and add **ed** and **ing**.

| tap | tapp**ed** | tapp**ing** |
| beg | begg**ed** | begg**ing** |

4 Words with more than one syllable, ending in a single consonant. If the stress is on the last syllable, double the consonant.

| propel | propel**led** | propel**ling** |

If the stress is not on the last syllable, just add **ed** and **ing.**

benefit	benefit**ed**	benefit**ing**
budget	budget**ed**	budget**ing**
sharpen	sharpen**ed**	sharpen**ing**

5 Words ending in – **l**. If there is only a single vowel before the –**l**, add **led** and **ling**:

| compel | compel**led** | compel**ling** |

If there is a double vowel before the —**l** , just add **ed** and **ing**:

| coil | coil**ed** | coil**ing** |
| peel | peel**ed** | peel**ing** |

6 Words ending in –**y**. If the letter before the –**y** is a vowel, just add **ed** and **ing**.

play	play**ed**	play**ing**
Exceptions		
lay	→	laid
pay	→	paid
say	→	said

If the letter before the –**y** is a consonant, change the **y** to an **i** before adding **ed**.

| cry | cr**ied** | cry**ing** |

Adding – ly

We can turn adjectives into adverbs by adding **ly** :
He is a quick worker : he works quick**ly**.
Usually you just add **ly** to the adjective, but there are
some exceptions.

1 If the word ends – **ll**, just add **y**.

full	→	full**y**

2 If a word of two or more syllables ends in –**y**, cut
off the **y** and add **ily**.

happ**y**	→	happ**ily**

3 One syllable words ending in –**y** are usually
regular.

shy	→	shy**ly**

Exceptions
gay	→	gai**ly**
day	→	dai**ly**

4 If the word ends in – **le**, cut off the **e** and add **y**.

simple	→	simpl**y**

Using ie / ei

The rule is : '**i** before **e** except after **c**, when the
sound is long ee.'

thi**ef**	re**ce**ive
pi**e**ce	**ce**iling

Exceptions

s**ei**ze	w**ei**r	w**ei**rd

Using ce / se

The rule is '**c** for a noun and **s** for a verb'.
(Easy to remember because the letters are in
alphabetical order: **C N**oun **S V**erb)

noun	**verb**
advi**ce**	advi**se**
practi**ce**	practi**se**
licen**ce**	licen**se**

Example :

I need your advi**ce**: will you advi**se** me?

Words that are easily confused

accept	except	
affect	effect	
aloud	allowed	
bail	bale	
bear	bare	
birth	berth	
board	bored	
chose	choose	
diary	dairy	
great	grate	
heel	heal	
here	hear	
lose	loose	
made	maid	
meter	metre	
miner	minor	
new	knew	
no	know	
pain	pane	
pair	pear	pare
past	passed	
peace	piece	
quite	quiet	
read	reed	
red	read	
right	write	
sew	sow	
some	sum	
stationary	stationery	
steak	stake	
tale	tail	
there	their	they're
threw	through	
to	two	too
wait	weight	
weak	week	
weather	whether	wether
where	wear	
were	we're	
which	witch	
whose	who's	
wood	would	
your	you're	

Single and double letters

A common spelling problem concerns words with single and /or double letters. Here is a list of the most common words which cause problems:

accelerate	imitate
address	immediate
assist	marvel
harass	mattress
beginning	millionaire
brilliant	necessary
caterpillar	occasion
collapse	parallel
collect	patrol
commit	pedal
corridor	possess
disappear	sheriff
discuss	success
embarrass	sufficient
exaggerate	terrible
happiness	unnecessary
illustrate	woollen

Other problem words

adaptation (not adaption)
computer
conjuror
connection
conqueror
conscience
conscious
encyclopedia
forty
grandad
granddaughter
miniature
moustache
rhyme
rhythm
somersault
wagon
yoghurt

Useful words

accent the way in which a person pronounces words is described as their accent. Everybody speaks with some kind of accent. If the accent belongs to a particular part of the country, it is called a regional accent. People sometimes talk about a 'posh' or 'BBC' accent. This is correctly called 'received **pronunciation**'. Accent is different from **dialect**.

adjective adjectives work with **nouns**. They help to make the meaning of the noun clearer or fuller. In these examples the adjectives are *marked out:*

I like reading *exciting* books.
I'm looking for an *old, green, rusty* bicycle.
Peter is very *happy* today.

adverb adverbs work with verbs, adjectives or other adverbs. They help to make their meaning clearer or fuller.

Working with verbs :
He walked *slowly* down the road.
Working with adjectives :
I am feeling *extremely* happy today.
Working with other adverbs:
The car came towards her *agonisingly* slowly.

apostrophe see page 179

article the words *a, an, the.*

audience the person (or people) you are speaking to, or writing for.

autobiography a **biography** that someone writes about themselves.

biography the story of a person's life.

borrowing see **loan word.**

casual (language) when we are speaking to (or writing for) people we know well, we use **vocabulary** and **grammar** that are less **formal** than when we are speaking to people we do not know well. For example we might say to a friend, 'Hang on a bit', while to a stranger we would say, 'Wait a minute.'

character a person in a story, poem or play

clause a group of words that contains a complete verb and makes sense. These are examples of clauses. (The verb is marked in each one):

As I *was going* up the stair,
I *met* a man
who *was*n't there.

colon the punctuation mark : . It is used to introduce a list, a saying, or a statement.

'We only have one rule in this school: treat others as you would like them to treat you.'

comma see page 178.

command see **sentence types.**

conjunction conjunctions are words that join other words together. In particular they join phrases and clauses:

I like walking along the beach *and* eating ice cream.
I only saw the bomb *when* I was nearly on top of it.

dialect the form of a language used in a particular area (regional, local dialect) or by a particular group of people (social dialect). Different dialects use different vocabulary and grammar. See page 140.

draft when we are writing something it often goes through a number of stages: we write it, read it through, think about it and rewrite it or alter it. Each version of the writing is called a draft.

drafting writing more than one **draft** of something. See page 174.

exclamation see **sentence types**

exclamation mark see page 177.

fiction something that is made up. See page 146.

first (language)   the language that we are brought up to speak at home. It is sometimes called the mother tongue. For most in Britain this is English, but many have a different first language: for example Gujarati, or Turkish.

foreign (language)   a language that is not generally spoken in a country. People learn it because they want to travel or work abroad. For example in Britain French and German are foreign languages.Foreign languages are often taught in schools.

formal (language)   when we are speaking to (or writing for) people whom we do not know well, we use language that is formal. We pay more careful attention to the grammar of our sentences and we use vocabulary that we know anyone will find acceptable. See **casual**.

full stop   see page 177.

grammar   grammar tells us how the words of a language are combined to make sentences. In English this is done by *word order* and *changing the form of words*:

word order : 'I saw Peter yesterday.' is an English sentence. 'Yesterday saw Peter I.' isn't.

changing the form of words : the verb 'see' changes to 'saw'. We say 'I saw Peter yesterday.' and not 'I see Peter yesterday.'

inverted comma   see page 181.

loan word   a word which is borrowed from another language. In English cafe is a borrowing from French, bungalow is a borrowing from Gujarati

narrative   writing or talking that tells the story of something that happened. A narrative may be true, or it may be fiction.

narrator   the person who tells the story.

non-standard   using vocabulary or grammar in ways that are not correct for **Standard English**.

noun   nouns are words that refer to people, places, things and ideas: cake, thought, child, sand, butter, happiness, November.

novel   a story that takes up a whole book. A novel usually has a number of **characters** and the events in it take place in one or more **settings**.

object   in many sentences, the object comes after the verb. It refers to the person or thing that is affected by the action of the verb:

The dog bit *the postman.*
I've lost *the notebook with my maths homework in it.*

phrase   a group of words that makes sense, but not full sense on its own. A phrase does not contain a complete verb. Examples:

coffee ice cream
playing football
the biggest aspidistra in the world.
See **clause**.

plot   the main events in a story and the way in which they are linked together.

point of view   when something happens it can be reported in different ways according to who is telling the story. For example if Mark and Imran have a row, Mark's version of what happened will be different from Imran's. If we are making up a story, we can choose to tell it from different points of view.

preposition   prepositions come before nouns and adverbs. They are the 'little words' of English :

up the hill, *by* now, *for* example, *until* then.

pronoun   pronouns are used to stand instead of nouns. They help us to avoid too much repetition. Some of the commonest pronouns are:

I, she, he, you, we, they, it,
me, her, him, us, them,
my, his, our, your, their, its,
myself, himself, herself, ouselves, yourselves, themselves, itself,
who, whom, whose, that, what, which,
this, that, these, those.

pronunciation   the way in which a person speaks the words of a language.

proof-reading reading through something that someone has written and correcting all the mistakes of spelling, punctuation and grammar.

prose writing in ordinary sentences. Prose is different from **verse** or poetry.

pun a play on words. Often words have more than one meaning (or two different words are pronounced in the same way) and we can make jokes by playing with these meanings. 'Knock knock' jokes often use puns:

> Knock knock
> Who's there ?
> Rice Crispies
> Rice Crispies who ?
> I'll tell you next week, it's a cereal.

purpose how we write or speak is affected by the **audience** and the purpose we have: why we are writing or speaking to them and the effect we want to have on them.

question see **sentence types.**

question mark see page 177.

rhyme when two words end with a similar sound pattern, they rhyme: for example bit/hit, house/grouse, examination/complication. Rhyme is often used in poetry.

role play see page 134.

second (language) some countries have several different first languages. So that people with different first languages can talk to each other, they have to learn a common second language. (For example in India Hindi and English are many people's second language. In Britain people who do not have English as their first language, usually have it as their second language.)

sentence types there are four main types of sentence:

> *Statement* : This is a statement.
> *Question* : What is the question ?
> *Command* : Do it straight away!
> *Exclamation* : What a wonderful idea that was !

setting the time and place where a story happens.

short story a story that is much shorter than a novel. Often short stories are short enough to be read at a sitting.

slang casual language that is special to one group of people. (Examples of this are school slang, thieves slang, motorbike slang.)It is often not acceptable outside that group. If you use slang outside the proper group you may well be criticised or laughed at.

spoonerism mixing up the first letters of words. (For example, saying 'a blushing crow' instead of 'a crushing blow'.)

Standard English the **dialect** of English that should be used when speaking in formal situations, and normally in writing.

statement see **sentence types.**

subject the subject of a sentence tells us what it is about. In a statement sentence it comes at the beginning:

> *Miriam* is unhappy.
> *The big blue book on the table* is mine.

syllable words can be made up of one or more syllables. Roughly speaking you can work out how many syllables a word has by counting the number of 'beats' as you say it:

> 1 syllable - bat, school, bounced
> 2 syllables - batted, bouncing
> 3 syllables - unbuttoned, Barnstaple

topic the subject matter of a piece of speech or writing.

verb it is difficult to write a proper sentence without a complete verb. Most verbs will fit into one or more of these spaces :

> He —————— it. (eg liked)
> She ——————. (eg is singing)
> It ————— good. (eg is)

verse writing that uses **rhyme** and rhythm.

vocabulary the words of a language, or a piece of speech or writing.

Acknowledgements

We are grateful to the following for permission to reprint copyright material:

John Agard: from *Mangoes and Bullets*, (Serpent's Tail), Copyright © 1985 by John Agard, by kind permission of Caroline Sheldon. **Steve Barlow and Steve Skidmore:** first published in this collection, by permission of the authors. **James Berry:** from *A Thief in the Village*, (Hamish Hamilton, 1987) Copyright © 1987 by James Berry, by permission of the publishers. **George Campbell:** from *First Poems*, (Garland, 1981), by permission of the publishers. **Charles Causley:** from *Collected Poems, 1951–1975*, (Macmillan), by permission of David Higham Associates. **Michael Croft:** from *Spare the Rod,* (Longman, 1953), by permission of Longman Group UK Ltd. **Berlie Doherty:** from *How green you are!* (Methuen, 1982), by permission of the publishers. **Olive Dove:** from *Drumming the Sky*, edited by Paddy Becheley, (BBC, 1981), by permission of the author. **Richard Edwards:** from *A Mouse in My Roof*, (Orchard, 1988), by permission of The Watts Group, publishers. **Gavin Ewart:** from *The Deceptive Grin of the Gravel Porters*, (London Magazine Editions), by permission of the author. **Nicholas Fisk:** from *Living Fire and Other SF Stories*, (Corgi, 1987), © Nicholas Fisk, 1987. All Rights Reserved. By permission of Transworld Publishers Ltd. **Judith Gorog:** from *A Taste for Quiet*, text copyright © 1982 by Judith Gorog, by permission of Philomel Books. **R Grant, N Thomas and P Williams:** from *The Puffin BMX Handbook*, (Puffin, 1984), by permission of Penguin Books Ltd. **Willis Hall:** from *Spooky Rhymes*, (Hamlyn), by permission of London Management.. **Hergé:** from *The Adventures of Tintin – Red Rackham's Treasure*, (Magnet, 1978), © Herge Casterman, English text © Methuen, 1959, by permission of Hergé Casterman and Methuen and Co. Ltd. **Andrew Langley:** from *At The Local Radio Station*, (Wayland, 1983), by permission of the publishers. **Dennis Lee:** from *Alligator Pie*, (Macmillan of Canada, 1974), © 1974 Dennis Lee, by permission of McKnight, Gosewich Associates Agency Inc. **Lara Mair:** from *Cadbury's Sixth Book of Children's Poetry*, (Beaver, 1988), by permission of Cadbury Schweppes. **Trevor Millum:** first published in *Warning: Too Much Schooling Can Damage Your Health*, (E J Arnold), by permission of the author. **Alfred Noyes:** from *Collected Poems*, by permission of John Murray (Publishers) Ltd. **Gareth Owen:** from *Salford Road*, (Collins, 1988), Copyright © 1986, 1988 by Gareth Owen, by permission of Rogers, Coleridge and White Ltd. **Michael Park:** 'Shaggy Dog Story' first published in *Scarborough Top Trader*, 22 September 1988, by permission of the author. **Brian Patten:** from *Gargling with Jelly*, (Viking, 1985), by permission of the author. **Philippa Pearce:** 'Auntie' © 1986 by Philippa Pearce from *Who's Afraid*, (Viking, 1986), by permission of Laura Cecil. **Susan Price:** from *Here Lies Price*, (1987), by permission of Faber and Faber Ltd. **William Scammell:** by permission of the author. **Shel Silverstein:** from *Where the Sidewalk Ends*, (Jonathan Cape), by permission of the author and publishers. **Christopher Somerville:** from *South Sea Stories*, (W H Allen, 1985), Copyright © Christopher Somerville, 1985, reprinted by permission of Richard Scott Simon Ltd. **Catherine Storr:** from *Cold Marble*, (1985), by permission of Faber and Faber Ltd. **Robert Swindells:** from *A Serpent's Tooth*, (Hamish Hamilton, 1988). Copyright © 1988 Robert Swindells, by permission of the publishers. **Kit Wright:** from *Cat Among the Pigeons*, (Viking Kestrel, 1987), Copyright © Kit Wright, 1984, 1987, by permission of Penguin Books Ltd.Extract from *Mizz*, April 1989, by permission of IPC Magazines Ltd/W.P.N.Extract from *The Innovations Report*, Autumn 1989, by permission of Innovations Ltd.Extract from *Which?*, August 1989, by permission of the Consumers' Association.Extract from *World of the Unkown: Monsters* by kind permission of Usborne Publishing Ltd, London.

Although every effort has been made to trace and contact copyright holders before publication, we have not been successful in a few cases. If notified, the publishers will be pleased to rectify any omissions at the earliest opportunity.

The illustrations are by:
Tony Ansell p.132, 166, 167; **Alex Ayliffe** p.150;
Jill Barton p.10, 13, 15, 17, 54; **Frances Cony** p.140, 141;
Martin Chatterton p.8, 48, 146, 147, 156, 157, 168, 169;
Katey Farrell p.55, 56, 128, 129, 149, 158;
John Levers p.67, 102, 104, 105, 110, 112, 113, 136, 138, 139, 144, 145;
Tania Lomas p.148; **Dom Mansell** p. 114, 116, 118, 162, 171, 174, 175;
Peter Melnyczuk p.28; **Jackie Morris** p.72, 74, 75;
Mike Nicholson p.36, 38, 39; **Mark Oldroyd** p.29;
Nicki Palin p.20-27; **Fiona Powers** p.58, 60, 61, 64;
Julie Roberts p.50-53; **Liz Roberts** p.57; **Rachel Ross** p.96, 98, 101;
Alan Rowe p.6, 7, 9, 31, 32, 33, 142, 143; **Nick Sharratt** p.130, 160,161;
Duncan Storr p.42-47; **Margaret Theakston** p.88-95, 154, 159, 170;
Martin Ursell p.76-83; **Barry Wilkinson** p.120, 122.

The publishers would like to thank the following for permission to reproduce
photographs:

Images Colour Library p.34; **Marshall Cavendish Picture Library** p.119;
Archie Miles p.85 (left & right); **Oxford Scientific Films** p.84;
John Seely p.135, 165 (right), 172,173;
Viewfinder Colour Photo Library p.164, 165 (left);
John Walmsley p.170, 171.
The cover photograph is reproduced by permission of Sinclair Stammers/ Science
Photo Library.

Although every effort has been made to trace and contact copyright holders before
publication, we have not been successful in a few cases. If notified, the publishers will
be pleased to rectify any omissions at the earliest opportunity.

Oxford University Press, Walton Street, Oxford OX2 6DP

Oxford New York Toronto
Delhi Bombay Calcutta Madras Karachi
Petaling Jaya Singapore Hong Kong Tokyo
Nairobi Dar es Salaam Cape Town
Melbourne Auckland

and associated companies in
Berlin Ibadan

Oxford is a trade mark of Oxford University Press

© John Seely, Frank Green, David Kitchen 1990
First published 1990
Reprinted 1990, 1991, 1992

ISBN 0 19 831161 3

Printed and bound in Great Britain by
Butler & Tanner Ltd, Frome and London